GW01465213

Never Alone

The remarkable story of

David & Robyn Claydon

Never Alone

The remarkable story of

David & Robyn Claydon

Cecily Paterson

SPCK
AUSTRALIA

NEVER ALONE: The remarkable story of David & Robyn Claydon
Copyright © 2006 Cecily Paterson

All rights reserved. Apart from any fair dealing for the purposes of private study, research, criticism or review as permitted under the Copyright Act, no part of this book may be reproduced or published by any process without the prior written permission of the publisher.

Cataloguing in publication data

Paterson, Cecily Anne.
Never alone : the remarkable story of David & Robyn Claydon.

ISBN 978 1 876106 13 3
ISBN 1 876106 13 1

1. Claydon, David.
2. Claydon, Robyn.
3. Missionaries - Australia - Biography.
4. Christian life.
I. Society for Promoting Christian Knowledge (Australia)

266.0092

Published in 2006 by
SPCK-Australia Publishing
Box 190 Rundle Mall Post Office,
Adelaide. South Australia 5000
publishing@spcka.org.au
www.spcka.org.au

Design - Cogdell Design & Fine Art
Printed by Hyde Park Press

ACKNOWLEDGEMENTS

Thank you to the many people who patiently answered my questions: Bob Adams, Bill Andersen, Jill Anstey, John Bales, Kim Barker, Geoff and Dearnne Bartlett, Peter and Terry Blowes, Frances Boland, Jane Chetty, Peter Chiswell, Harold Dews, Dudley Foord, Harry Goodhew, Bill Graham, Kevin Harper, Alan Hohne, Wendy Hill, Alan Kerr, Victor Kijvanit, Denis and Anne McIntyre, John Menear, Eva Mrsic, Roger Parrott, David Parsons, John Reid, Margaret Simpson, Evangeline Sita, Janine Stewart, Beth and Bob Sutton, St Matthew's West Pennant Hills office staff, Sue Talbot and Olga Zaprometova.

It has been a tremendous privilege to be entrusted with the details of your lives, David and Robyn. I can only hope that I have done some small amount of justice to your stories; but, more importantly, to the story of God working in you and through you.

Thank you to Margaret and Ross, whose childminding talents allowed me to type freely without disturbance. Thank you too, to the rest of my family for listening as I've talked it all out with you.

Special love to two dear men: to my father John, who has always encouraged me to tell stories, and to my husband Andrew, whose optimism allows me to take on crazy challenges, never questioning whether I'll succeed or not.

CONTENTS

CHAPTER ONE

A BABY IS BORN, FOUND, AND SAVED

Somewhere, sometime, a baby was born. Exactly where and when, no-body knows for sure.

Who the parents were, what could be known of their history, their character and their story, disappeared after the birth of their child, never to be found again.

But their child remained; for his first few years an anonymous orphan in a tiny British orphanage in Palestine. As alone as he seemed, this child growing up in a country which was not his own, spoke a language which was not his own, and had no friends to speak of. But his story shows how, even in his youngest days, he was never alone. God already had him in the palm of his hand, with plans to do him good and not to harm him.

It is not the normal beginning to a story of a remarkable person, used by a remarkable God. Most biographies start with the family history of their subject: how their parents met, the character of their grandparents, the siblings born to the family, and the either happy and secure, or difficult and poverty-infested earliest years.

In the case of the earliest years of David (and he had no surname at this early stage), we must come to the Bethlehem Babies' Home in the late 1930s, where 22 orphaned or abandoned children slept in a dormitory, sat in rows on their potties, and played games in the olive orchard and orange groves.

Even though the orphanage was run by the British Protectorate government in Palestine, and the matron was a German lady, David was the only English baby amongst 21 Arabic babies and infants, and all the children grew up speaking Arabic together. David's first language and first cultural attitudes were Arabic.

It was not a peaceful time in Palestine. Britain had been granted a mandate over Palestine in 1920, and had expressed the desire to establish a homeland for the Jewish people. Hostilities between Arabs and Jews began very soon, and the British found themselves in the middle, trying to keep opposing forces apart. In 1936, the conflicts worsened. British forces were targeted by both Arabs and Jews and terrorist activities increased. The unending conflicts have continued to this day.

The main road from Jerusalem to Bethlehem ran by the orphanage, and the frequent army convoys passing triggered the orphanage children to play a game of 'searching for the enemy'. As David looked different from his Arabic friends, he was designated the 'enemy'. His playmates locked him between the window glass and the wooden shutters, so that the 'army' couldn't find him!

Times were tough in these pre-war days, and David's memories of the orphanage are filled with rice meals. It is doubtful if they had much else to eat, apart from olives and oranges which grew behind the buildings. But their young lives were relatively untouched by the troubles brewing around them, and they would have had little idea that their orphanage home and domestic life, such as it was, was about to come to an end.

In Europe war had broken out, and the Protectorate Government had been ordered by Westminster to intern all Germans by placing them in detention camps. Post World War I, there were many Germans in Palestine, and whole families were eventually detained in camps. As the matron of the orphanage was German, she was set for internment, and the orphanage was listed to be wound up.

A British Government social worker, Miss Lora Claydon, had been appointed to take over the management of the Babies' Home, with a view to finding homes for the children and shutting it all down. She first visited the orphanage in October 1939 and set to work at some stage after that.

Miss Claydon was a Christian lady of faith, verve and a heartfelt love for little children. She had been a CMS missionary in India for some years before she arrived in Palestine and was fluent in Urdu, so she could understand a little bit of the related Arabic language, although she couldn't speak it. She began to identify the children, look for their relatives and persuade the extended families to take in their nephews and nieces and make new homes for them.

As she listed the children, however, she found one child with no documentation at all. No birth certificate, no papers as to his parents' identity, his birth place, or even his age. David was a child with no known extended family and no links in the world. She was successful in finding homes for the Arabic children, but no-one wanted a white-skinned English boy to join their family, even if he could speak and swear in Arabic as well as any other boy!

Miss Claydon's progress in finding homes for the children was hampered in 1940 by an outbreak of measles at the orphanage. What one small child contracts will quickly spread to others, and soon every remaining child in the Babies' Home, including David, had the measles. The children were taken by bus to the German Hospital in Jerusalem and admitted to hospital, two to a bed.

Unfortunately, conditions at the German Hospital were not good. As all Germans were slowly being arrested and detained, the staff morale was low, and patient care had become a low priority. On her first visit to her young charges in hospital, Miss Claydon found little David very sick indeed. He had contracted double pneumonia due to a lack of proper care and had lapsed into a coma. She could see that no-one in the hospital was going to do anything substantial to help him, so she grabbed a blanket, wrapped him up and took him in a taxi straight up the road to the CMJ Mission Hospital.

CMJ is the 'Church's Ministry among the Jews', and the CMJ Hospital, on the Street of the Prophets, was staffed by two Christian missionary doctors. Miss Claydon and the doctors prayed for little

David, still in a coma, and Miss Claydon spent the next couple of weeks getting all the Christians she knew to pray for him.

His life hung in the balance for two weeks, but all of their prayers were answered, and David survived.

It would be his first escape from death.

By the time David recovered, in mid-1940, and was well enough to leave the hospital, this four year old boy had another problem of survival to face. The orphanage had closed down and all the children had been sent to other homes. Miss Claydon had found nowhere for him to go and did not know what to do with him.

For several years Lora Claydon had felt a strong call of God on her life to go to Palestine to work with babies and little children, but many of her plans had been frustrated. Now she found herself in a situation where a little boy was dependent on her and her alone. Perhaps it was the two weeks of intense prayer that bonded her to him, or perhaps she just felt sorry for him and thought he was gorgeous with his red hair and magnetic eyes, or perhaps it was because of prayer and guidance from her Daily Light Bible readings, that very soon Lora decided to become David's guardian and took him to live with her.

CHAPTER TWO

THE INS AND OUTS OF MISS LORA CLAYDON

When Lora Claydon first saw David, she was 46 years old. She had been born in Burwood, Sydney, in August 1893, the third daughter for her committed Christian parents Ernest and Eleonore Claydon. Ernest, a stern, aloof man, was a civil engineer before he felt a strong call to be a clergyman, and was ordained an Anglican priest in 1895. He took his parish work very seriously, and there were certain times that he was not to be disturbed, particularly on Saturdays when he was 'sermonising'.

His wife was no less serious, but perhaps warmer and more comfortable. She kept an open home and was very involved in parish work, despite producing growing numbers of little Claydons. Her eleven children were born one every 18 months to two years!

Lora, as one of the elder children, was called on to help with the younger ones, but it was the particular task of her eldest sister, Crystal, to look after the babies. As each baby was weaned, he or she was given to Crystal to care for at night.

Understandably Crystal wasn't always happy about it. Once, as a teenager, she was unaware that yet another baby was on the way. On the day of the birth, the children were all sent out for a picnic. When they returned, Crystal was asked to go upstairs to her mother's room to see the new baby. Astonished and furious, she stormed upstairs and told Eleonore, "We don't want any more babies. There are too many already."

The children were brought up in a Christian household, and took their faith very seriously. All of them were given a healthy dose of missionary commitment, particularly in supporting the

Church Missionary Society[1]. Missionary ardour was an important part of evangelical church life in the early part of the twentieth century, and the Claydons took it on themselves to serve on committees and promote the ministry of CMS in Australia.

CMS was almost like an extended family for the Claydons, so it was a special privilege for Ernest and Eleonore to have two daughters and one son become missionaries to India.

The first of these was Lora. At the age of 23, this independent, determined young single woman had a strong missionary call, and entered Deaconess House in Sydney for training in 1916. Finally, in November 1917, CMS deemed her ready to start her missionary work, and sent her out on a ship to India. Lora's fledgling missionary career was on its way.

Her first posting was a few months in Karachi, the major port city now of Pakistan, where she studied the Urdu language. When her teacher arrived, he presented his card, which was also his certificate of qualification. Under his name was printed 'Triple Fail, B.A.'. For some reason, Lora engaged him! They got along well, and before long, she was stumbling along in a conversation about her journey to India from Australia, via Singapore. He was impressed, but his English was about as good (or bad) as Lora's elementary Urdu, and he summed her up, perhaps prophetically, by saying, "You are a very travelsome lady".

Despite the 'triple fail', Lora passed her language exam at the end of the year. In October 1918 she was sent up to Amritsar, now on the Indian side of the border of Pakistan and India.

Lora was not to know it, but her time in Amritsar would be the beginning of her difficulties as a missionary, and the eventual cause of her resignation from CMS.

---

[1] CMS, which is still going strong today, was an Anglican missionary sending body, which began in England in 1799 through the efforts of prominent evangelicals such as William Wilberforce and John Newton.

To begin with, almost as soon as she arrived she contracted small-pox. She had been immunized for it nine months previously, but in those days immunizations were not always effective, and she became extremely ill for about two months. Small-pox was a disease of great concern; not many recovered from it, and most were scarred for life. Lora's friends and supporters were praying for her recovery, and despite a badly pocked face, she did get better and went back to work.

Political troubles were the next thing to lay her low. Massive riots in Amritsar in 1919 put an end to normal life for everyone for a period. Many were killed and fled the city. Shops, schools and hospitals closed down for a while. Lora and her British CMS workmate at one point were holed up in a shelter, hiding from the mêlée.

For someone used to the relative peace and order of Sydney, in a foreign country and away from family and friends, this was a very difficult time. The shock and trauma had a taxing effect on her. Debriefing or counselling of any sort was unknown in those days; good missionaries were expected to pray, hold their heads up and get on with their work and keep any ill effects to themselves, so that's what Lora did – for a little while at least.

She moved on to do village work in Tarn Taran, but with an immunity probably dampened by the small-pox, ill health continued to follow her, and four fairly major episodes of dysentery and malaria slowed her down, plus a three-week bout of dengue fever. For someone as conscientious, dedicated and clever as Lora, this sickness was frustrating and would have caused her to question her whole purpose in being in India. When she did recover, her hardworking upbringing took over and she continually overcommitted herself, taking on more than she could realistically chew.

It was from this point that her missionary career became a

regular pattern of over-hard work and praise-worthy results, followed by nervousness, exhaustion and depression, followed in turn by extra-long periods of rest and recovery.

Lora was a good missionary. She truly loved God, related well to people and worked hard. But she was also not a good missionary. She lacked balance, couldn't pace herself, and was severely affected by the traumas she had experienced in Amritsar.

Three times she was sent back to Australia for extra-long furloughs[2] to recover. In 1925, one doctor wrote that she was 'anaemic, nervous and 'utterly unfit' for her work'.[3] Her symptoms showed what many doctors today would diagnose as depression or anxiety, with irritability, sleeplessness, impaired appetite and nervousness.[4]

The CMS committees found themselves in a quandary about Lora after her third furlough in 1933. Should they send her back? Was she up to it? Lora herself was keen to return: missionary work was still her first love, and her true calling; she believed her health would be fine. But the CMS secretary in India thought otherwise and cabled the reply that, "owing to Claydon's temperament, cannot guarantee health." Lora would have to wait to go back, for the foreseeable future.

It was a blow. But Lora was never without a plan for long and made spur of the moment decisions very easily. She loved to travel and an enforced break would be a good time to visit relatives and siblings in England. More importantly, it would be a great opportunity to indulge one of her long-held desires, to visit Palestine – the 'Holy Land'.

Asking for, and getting six months leave without pay from CMS, she set off, sailing third class steerage, halfway around the world.

---

[2] Most missionaries would have spent 6 to 9 months on 'furlough' in Australia, resting and speaking to church groups about their work.
[3] Letter from Dr Franklin, Lahore October 1926.
[4] Letter from Dr Playe, Melbourne February 1928

Lora's independent personality meant that she could always find something to do, and some way to achieve what she wanted. But the flip side meant that she was not very attentive to administrative detail. And because of this quirk in her personality, Lora's relationship with CMS began to deteriorate.

After a flying visit to Palestine, she arrived in England. A medical check a few months later found her still unfit to return to India, and so she quickly took a job with the Bermondsey Medical Mission as a social and spiritual worker.

Even though she was earning a salary, she then wrote off to CMS in Australia asking for a pension, back-paid from the time she left Australia. CMS was a little shocked. To begin with, Lora was on leave without pay at her own request; she had not written to them telling them any details about her new job; and it was common knowledge that CMS only paid pensions to those who had worked as CMS missionaries for 30 years or more.[5]

Lora never responded to their reply, and over the next year or two, a variety of letters from CMS Australia informed her that she would have to resign as a missionary, as she had a job and as her health was inadequate to return to India. Lora's replies were unclear, sporadic and contradictory. She couldn't see that she needed to resign; indeed she may have felt like she was losing her family if she did.

The toing and froing about her resignation caused quite a headache in the CMS Sydney office. On one hand it was simple: Lora would have to resign as she could not return to India; on the other hand, she didn't want to, and the Claydon family had plenty of clout in the running of CMS. However, Lora's missionary service with CMS was finally put to rest in April 1936 when CMS England recorded her resignation.

---

[5] CMS policy has since changed and all missionaries are credited with a resettlement fund.

Meanwhile, her work at the Bermondsey Medical Mission had been very fruitful. Ever innovative, she pioneered a social work department[6] and had plenty of opportunity for evangelism and Christian ministry.

But the call of the Holy Land was becoming greater, and her desire to be in missionary work had never gone away. One particular idea was gradually gaining strength in her mind - to start a Babies' Home in Jerusalem.

So in November 1937, Lora sailed at her own expense for Palestine. As usual, she had limited funds (only £100), but plenty of ideas and plenty of faith. The Babies' Home was to be attached to a hospital and school and was to be self-supporting, completely independent of CMS.[7] She had connections, plans and enthusiasm; her health seemed to be adequate for her task; the only thing she lacked was a regular income for herself. Unfortunately, this detail was a bit of a glitch in her plan. Her visa to stay in Palestine was completely dependent upon her having enough to live on – at a minimum of £1000 pounds.

So Lora started to write letters. As CMS Australia was 'family' in her mind, she couldn't see why it wouldn't help, and pay her a pension that she still believed she was owed, despite having been assured several times that she was not entitled to it.

She wrote, pleading her case: "There is no Protestant home for children. Several people who are in touch with the work as a whole have begged me to start this venture... I believe God has called me here... I am therefore asking CMS for the pension due to me for the period of service 1917-32...."[8]

It was another headache for CMS Australia, and they had to refuse her. Lora's plans were frustrated again. Without the income or

[6] Sir Marcus Loane in his funeral eulogy for Lora Claydon.
[7] Letter from Secretary of CMS Jerusalem to CMS Australia March 1938.
[8] Letter from Lora Claydon to CMS Australia August 1938.

support she needed for her venture, her visa ran out and she had to return to England in September 1938.

As ever, she was not a woman who would take no for an answer, and it is testament to her persuasive and charming personality that she was able to convince the General Secretary of CMS England, as well as an Australian clergyman, Rev Leyland Parsons, to write to CMS Australia on her behalf, again putting the same request.

Parsons wrote in her support: "Miss Claydon is a fine type of missionary," and the CMS England General Secretary said, "She is doing a very fine bit of work in Bethlehem." But CMS Australia was unpersuaded, and again paid her nothing.[9]

The Babies' Home scheme seemed fruitless, and Lora was without a purpose or job again. The frustrations at every turn may have been surprising and disappointing for her, but she still had one thing going for her – a great deal of faith, and a very strong knowledge of God's call on her life; specifically at this moment, to work with babies in Palestine.

And God came through for her. At some stage over the next few months, Lora managed to find a job with the British Protectorate Government as a social worker, winding up the Bethlehem Babies' Home. It brought her back to Palestine some time before World War II broke out. And ultimately it brought her to David.

Despite the limitations of Lora's health, and the frailties of her personality, God's plans overruled, as they always do. Lora's heartfelt desire to shelter babies in Palestine brought her to rescue one particular little boy who would be part of God's plan for his world in the future.

---

[9] Even though the CMS committees would not support Lora in any official way, she was not their enemy. The General Secretary of CMS Sydney wrote very kindly at the end of his letter of refusal: "I do trust that you are keeping well. I have happy memories of our two interviews, when you certainly were a spiritual medicine to me!"

CHAPTER THREE

DAVID SETTLES IN AND LORA GOES AWAY

Taking on a young boy of nearly four, who had never lived in a family situation before, would be a challenge for anyone, but Lora Claydon had a few extra difficulties to contend with when she took on the guardianship of David.

To begin with, they didn't speak the same language. Although she was fluent in Urdu from her years in India, and she could understand and read a little Arabic, speaking it was another matter. David spoke only Arabic, so Lora hired a 14-year old Arabic boy to translate for her and care for David while she was working.

Her second challenge was David's Arabic attitudes. This was another reason why she hired the young Arabic boy. Even at his tender age, David wouldn't take any instructions from a woman! In the first week she tried to make him obey her, but, as he says "any well-trained Arabic boy would do", he jumped up on the table and slapped her on the face.

Despite the challenges, Lora seemed to become attached to David, and took on the task of documenting their relationship and getting papers for him. Guardianship was an informal arrangement, and as she wanted to ensure she could take him with her to either Australia or England at the end of the war, she asked the British Protectorate Government to regard her as a guardian aunt, and named David with her family name. So on 27 September 1940, he was baptized David Claydon, a naturalized British (Palestinian) citizen.

However, he still did not have a birth date. Lora had been guessing his age from the time she saw him. She chose the fifth of October which had some significance for her and may possibly have been the first day she saw him in the orphanage.[1]

So now, at the age of four, this little boy had a name and a birthday, a guardian aunt and a ready-made family with relatives back in Australia and England. But he still had no clue as to where he came from or who his parents were.

In later years, he was told by people living in Jerusalem that his father was a British civil servant working with the Protectorate Government. They believed his parents were both killed in the cross-fire between Jewish, Arab and British soldiers in late 1936 or 1937. However, he never found out if the people who told him this actually knew his parents, and the information was never confirmed.

Records of British civil servants in Palestine around this time were in a government building in Jerusalem which was bombed in 1946 by Zionists. All the documentation was destroyed. Given Lora's lack of attention to administrative detail, it is likely that she never took the steps before this point which could have led to a better knowledge of David's parents.

So David never found out who his real family was, and, as he got older, he never cared to know. If his parents had had relatives in England, they had never, to his knowledge, made an effort to find him, and so he was not interested in finding out who they were. He was given the Claydon surname before he consciously knew or cared about surnames, and over the years came to identify with the Claydon family, love his Claydon cousins, and accept their family history as his own.

Now that Lora was officially David's guardian aunt, she had to re-think her strategy for both making a living and managing her

---

[1] Choosing this birth date still didn't solve the problem of exactly how old he was. In the end, a medical examination of the bones in his wrists when he was about seven established his approximate age. The doctor determined his birth to have occurred at some time in the latter half of 1936.

THE REMARKABLE STORY OF DAVID AND ROBYN CLAYDON

headstrong young charge. She was unable to continue working as a social worker for the British Government. But as always she was quick to grab an opportunity.

This time the opportunity came from a chance meeting with a relation of Emperor Haile Selassie of Ethiopia, the Viceroy of Abyssinia. This person was studying theology in the Ethiopian Orthodox Church college in Jerusalem.

The suggestion came up that Lora could take his three-year old son, Prince Taritu, to board with her and teach him English. Lora thought this would be an ideal solution to both her income problems and the need for David to learn English. (David himself thought it would be easier for Lora to learn Arabic!)

Lora resigned from her government post, rented a small house in Jericho, and Prince Taritu, nicknamed Tickitiboo, came to stay with her and David. For a little while two Czech boys, Svarrick and Dodo Haik, also joined the classes, and Lora and David lived off the fees from the boys' parents.

While the English lessons and the playmates might have been the ideal solution to part of Lora's problems, unfortunately the money was coming in less than regularly and Lora could not manage financially. While David's memories of this time are filled with a lot of fun, playing with the other boys, they are also filled with a constant lack of food. He and Lora depended on wild grapes and cheap Arabic pita bread to fill themselves up.

For all her lack of cash, however, Lora still had plenty of faith. Once, while they were walking down the street in Jericho to go to the shops for food, Lora had no money at all. She told David this, and they prayed that God would meet their needs. Sure enough, as they walked down the dusty road, a raven dropped a coin right in front of them. It was a shiny 50 mil piece, plenty for a day's rations. For the next few decades, David was very quick to see and grab coins dropped on the ground!

After about six months of teaching the boys, Lora was dissatisfied. It may have been her financial difficulties; perhaps she saw the need to save enough money to eventually take David back to England or Australia when it was safer to travel after the war, and she knew she would not earn enough by teaching the boys. Perhaps she was not convinced that her English teaching was very successful, with her charges seemingly slow to learn. It may simply have been the fact that she seemed to like to move on and try new things.

But for whatever reason, Lora negotiated with Prince Taritu's father and decided to take a job in Ethiopia, teaching English to the Emperor's children.

Strangely enough, even though she had just become his guardian aunt less than a year before, Lora did not take David with her. Instead, she left him in Jerusalem, for a period of about two years, living with a Christian doctor's family.

Lora's reasons must have seemed logical, or at least sensible to her, because in future years she never expressed any regret over leaving David. She had formalized all the guardianship documents, so she knew he was 'hers', she would be earning money which would take them both back to Australia eventually, and she was seeing an interesting, 'romantic' part of the world. David was perfectly well-provided for, living with a pleasant and good family, and learning English.

But for a small child with no parents, who had had a severe recent illness, and who was adjusting to a new guardian, a new home and a new language, it was another massive change, another jolt to the stability of life, and all of these changes would have a much larger effect on him than Lora would ever realize.

Dr Cyril Politian was one of the doctors who had looked after David in the CMJ Hospital during his coma at the age of four. He and his wife had one child, Mary, who was about two years older than David, and she took a genuine interest in this little boy who had come to stay. Mary cared about David, and her sisterly love for him started to change his supercilious attitude towards girls. David cannot remember any cross words of annoyance or anger between them. They shared secrets, discussed the problems of life (including how they could kill Hitler, if only they could get to him) and shared most of their illnesses, except for two!

David's health problems were by no means over at this point, although they were not as serious as previously. At about four and a half, he went back into the CMJ hospital to have his tonsils out. Hospitals can be scary places for little children, and David was frightened by the large bright light that was brought down above his face in the surgery.

After the operation, David spent some time recuperating in the children's ward. This was a room about 20 metres long, with beds lined up on each side, and, down the middle, a row of cots for babies and little children like David..

Apart from the doctors and nurses rounds, things in the children's ward only became exciting in the late afternoon, when lantern slides were projected onto the wall for the children to look at.[2]

As David watched the slides, he noticed one in particular. It was a gently coloured picture of a shepherd holding a lost lamb. As the person showing the slides told the parable, David was glued to the image.

"If Jesus cared about one orphan sheep, surely he cares about one orphan boy," he said to himself.

This was the first time David thought consciously of himself as an orphan. While he had the indefinable basic emotions of a small

[2] Lantern slides were the 'multi-media' presentations of the day and greatly loved by Sunday schools and missionaries on deputation for telling Bible stories and missionary adventures.

child up to this point, the lost lamb picture gave him more understanding of how he felt.

His feelings were given a beautiful outlet when, in hospital, David was given his first ever toy! In these days of western material wealth, it is almost inconceivable that a child would be four and a half before having even one toy to play with. But, recuperating in the children's ward, he was given a soft, grey felt kangaroo. From that point on, he took the kangaroo to bed with him every night, as if it were the lost lamb, and fell asleep talking to it and cuddling it for comfort.

On his recovery he went back to the Politians, to the loving companionship of Mary, and to the more remote care of 'Aunty Politian' as he called her. Aunty sometimes played shops with the children on wet days, but David has more memories of Uncle being involved with the children's games.

The days with the Politians were mostly filled with joy for little David. He loved Mary and spent fine days playing with her on the roof of the hospital apartment. In the evenings in the warmth of the bathroom, he and Mary kneeled at Aunty's lap to say their simple prayers. They then went to bed, Uncle reading them a chapter from Robinson Crusoe as they dozed off.

One of Lora's aims for leaving David with the Politians may have been for him to learn English. Unfortunately she and the Politians believed this could be best achieved by letting him lose all his Arabic. David was learning English but was still desperate to speak his mother tongue. However he was forbidden, on threat of smackings, to speak Arabic, and especially to talk to the Arabic-speaking hospital gatekeeper. He could sense his Arabic slipping away from him and for the rest of his life was sad that he was forced to forget a language which is so hard to learn as an adult.

During school terms, Mary and David attended the British Community School. This was David's first opportunity for formal schooling. This would have been a real boon for a bright little boy, but unfortunately his time at school was limited, as he was affected by another serious illness.

Having breakfast one morning, he felt the breakfast table start to swirl around. Uncle Politian picked him up just in time and took him to a basin to vomit. From there it was straight into a cot in a darkened bedroom with round-the-clock care, as he had a serious, nearly deadly case of sunstroke.

For the second time in his short life, he lapsed into a coma – this time for three months. There was little hope until a visiting missionary doctor administered a new 'wonder drug' together with a lot of prayer. If the drug didn't work, David was expected to die.

However, God's hand was still on this little orphan, and he had other plans for him. The prayers were answered, and David emerged out of his 'deep sleep', as he thought it was, not knowing what he was saying.

It was his second escape from an early death.

The war was intensifying in this period of 1941-42 when David was with the Politians, and it began to affect all of their lives more and more. The Germans were trying to take over North Africa and the Politians followed the battles and progress of the war every evening. Although the local radio station had been bombed by Zionists, a temporary facility was set up and every evening the radio would spring to life.

Children could hardly be sheltered from the widespread fighting which affected almost everyone in almost every part of the world. David and Mary would listen with Aunty and Uncle Politian to the broadcasts, and then look at the map they had pinned up on the wall next to the radio to mark the progress of the enemy and the Allies.

With constant air raids, the children became used to danger. The flat they lived in was built above the hospital Outpatients building, with an air raid shelter underneath. Bombings came from two sources: either German enemy aircraft, or small Zionist planes. When the attacks were staged by the Zionists, the Politians thought it was unlikely that a hospital caring for Jews would be targeted, so they stayed where they were and did not bother going down to the shelter.

In the mornings though, Mary and David liked to go down the street and survey the damage. They would look at buildings which had had their fronts sheared right off like dolls houses, so everyone could see into the rooms. David would try to imagine how people felt when their beds were left dangling over the edge of the floor.

One image that was engraved in his mind was that of an office building. Everything had been burnt out except the steel structure which was still standing, including a solitary steel spiral staircase. For him that staircase was a symbol of solitude and defiance in the midst of hopelessness. It became a picture of himself, seemingly alone in a hopeless world.

And David was quite alone. Even while he felt happy at the Politians, and loved Mary dearly, his status in the family was not assured. He never properly belonged to them, and he felt it.

Early on in his time with the family, just before he turned five, he was called in to see Uncle Politian. Uncle gave him a watch, and taught him how to tell the time.

"I'm giving you this," he said, "because you will be travelling on a ship to Eritrea to see your Aunty Lora. You have to be a good boy and do what the Captain says. The ship's nurse will look after you during the voyage."

David had no idea why he was being sent away, but he sat on the bed, dutifully going over and over how to tell the time while Uncle went to check some details. When he came back in he proclaimed that David wouldn't be going, as the ship had just been torpedoed in the Mediterranean ocean!

A few months later, this process was repeated, but this time David was being sent to England to be with Lora's Aunt Agnes.

Again, the ship was torpedoed on its way to Haifa and David was not able to go.

In 1943, Lora again arranged for David to travel to England on a ship, under the care of Doris Hawkins, the Matron of the CMJ Hospital. Matron Hawkins was engaged to take two children with her, David and a little girl of about two, Sally. At the last minute however, she decided she could only manage one child, and left David behind.

Tragically the ship was torpedoed just past the Straits of Gibraltar. Matron Hawkins was able to get to a lifeboat, but as she did so, little Sally fell out of her arms into the freezing sea and was drowned. The crew and passengers who did manage to get to the life boats were picked up by a German submarine and looked after, but then were put back out to sea again on their own. Many of them died from starvation and over-exposure. Matron Hawkins was the only woman survivor of the wreck.

So David again escaped death and tragedy, and lived to see another day.

But one day, in late 1943, all of this suddenly came to an end.

One afternoon Aunty Politian asked David to come into the dining room, where there was someone to see him. She wouldn't tell him who it was. As he walked through the doorway, he saw a white-haired lady sitting on a stool. He had no idea who she was, but she seemed to know his name.

"David, come here and sit beside me on the stool," she said to him in a strong voice, with a conservative English accent.

"I'm Lora Claydon. I'm your guardian, and I've come back to Jerusalem to look after you. You're going to come and live with me, and you can call me Aunty Lora."

CHAPTER FOUR

COLOUR AND SPICE – GROWING UP

Lora had been having a very interesting time in Ethiopia. She taught the Emperor's children English for a short time, and then, true to form, moved on to run a British primary school in Asmara, Eritrea, before returning to Jerusalem.[1]

Why did Lora come back when she did? It may have been because her job was finished; perhaps the school didn't need her anymore; perhaps someone more qualified had taken over; perhaps Lora herself lost interest.

Or perhaps her return was on the request of Mrs Politian. Lora told David, much to his dismay and disbelief, in later years, that Mrs Politian had never really wanted to have him stay with the family. This may have been the reason why her manner had always seemed remote and distant to him. She had probably agreed to take him only temporarily while Lora tried to arrange for him to be sent back to England to be with her relatives. After two years of caring for him, including several months when he was seriously ill, Mrs Politian probably realized that the efforts to send him elsewhere were going to come to nothing, and she may have asked Lora to return and take him off her hands.

As good temporary guardians, the Politians had made sure that they reminded David from time to time that Lora existed and that he would eventually go and live with her. But David had not known Lora for very long, and after two years without seeing her, an

---

[1] On her return from North Africa, Lora flew by DC3 to Cairo. The trip turned out to be a little more exciting than Lora had bargained for as the door opened while the plane was in mid-air. The attendant and co-pilot used every piece of material they could find to make a rope and tried to hook the door closed, but they didn't succeed. Thankfully the plane landed safely and no-one was hurt, but it did stop Lora ever flying again, even though she was an adventurous person.

eternity for a little boy of six, he had no real concept of who she was.

All he knew was that one day he lived with the Politians, and with his adored Mary, and the next day he had to pack his things and leave. It was difficult and confusing for him, and it wasn't made any easier by Lora. She had come straight from the railway station to get him and had her few possessions with her. They packed up David's things and left the Politians, but they had nowhere to go. Lora had not made any arrangements for a place to live, nor did she have any income. However, she still had plenty of faith in God, and the ability to live very simply, and she probably counted on the fact that 'something' would work out.

Obviously she needed money, so they went to Barclays Bank where she still had a small savings account. While they were standing in Barclays, the 'something' Lora was hoping for did work out. Mr AP Stanley Clark, the Barclays Regional Director for the Middle East, walked through the banking hall.

Mr Clark was a friend of Lora's; she had got to know him and his wife, a Christian couple, on her first long stay in Jerusalem. After a short conversation, he invited Lora and David to come and stay on the large property of his bank manager's home. They had a roof over their heads temporarily.

Temporary became permanent as, again, Mr Clark came in useful. He was the Chairman of the committee which cared for the 'Garden Tomb', commonly believed to be the tomb Jesus was buried in,[2] and he gave Lora the job of being warden of the property. So around May 1943 Lora and David moved to live in a tiny stone cottage in the Garden. Lora's main duties were to show visitors

---

[2] The garden tomb was known as 'Gordon's Cavalry and Garden Tomb' and was an area which a General Gordon had excavated, to discover a tomb with a rolling stone and a wine press, indicating it was a garden in Christ's era.
The garden had all the features that would have been expected of Joseph of Arimathea's garden and tomb, described in the Gospel of John. It was at the foot of a hill which looked like a large skull, before buildings sprang up around it.

around and to manage the gardener. There was no income attached to the job, but their accommodation was free, and visitors, usually army personnel on leave, would often make a donation, which Lora was entitled to keep.

Of course, money was still a problem. Even with the donations, there were many occasions when they had no money and were hungry.

"What can we do if we have no food to eat, Aunty Lora?" David asked one day.

"Well, in some places in India, when they don't have any food, they collect grass and cook that and eat it," Lora said matter-of-factly.

Even though her answer put David off the thought of India for life, it seemed quite a good solution, except for the small problem of it being a hot, dry summer at the time, with no grass around at all.

As always, prayer was Lora's constant recourse. On one cashless day, as Lora and David sat praying in the garden for enough money to be able to eat, David, who had not closed his eyes properly, noticed Mr Clark's chauffeur place an envelope in the letter box. He told Lora about it when she had finished praying and she sent him to get the letter. It had £10 in it – enough to last them a month!

Lora had the Claydon can-do attitude and decided to use her artistic skills for income. She had always loved art and painting, and produced some chalk and watercolour drawings - paintings of Biblical scenes and characters. The scenes were printed onto flannelette, and the characters cut out and stuck onto sandpaper. Using this type of 'flannelgraph set' was popular for story-telling in Sunday schools in those days. Lora sold her sets, called 'The Graphic Way', to visitors to the Garden Tomb, who were delighted to have them for their Sunday schools at home.

It was a slow and hard process though. It took about a month for Lora to complete a set, even using David as convenient labour, cutting out characters and sticking them onto the sandpaper. She sold them for what would have been the equivalent of around $20 these days, so it was not a lucrative proposition.

For this short period, David was attending the Jerusalem British School, but the war was continuing to make life in Jerusalem difficult, and, in July, the school shut down.

This, combined with the lack of funds, pushed Lora to move on again. In September 1943 she landed herself a job as a teacher, with both income and a house, at the English-speaking Tabeetha School[3] in Jaffa, the place the Bible knows as Joppa.[4]

All children, as they grow, have periods in their life of vivid memories, and this was David's time to look, observe and experience the excitement of life going on around him.

He was still suffering from the loss of his beloved Mary, but this grief was stilled a little by finding a new playmate. A British family living next door had a little girl about his age, and the pair adopted the old Christian cemetery close by as their own private playground.

In the warmer months, life was overtaken by blinding sandstorms. David probably enjoyed the experience of being covered

[3] The school was still operating as a Church of Scotland school in 1994, when David visited the Holy Land again and the head teacher at the time had been in David's class in 1943.

[4] Joppa was where Peter saw his vision which led to Gentiles being accepted as Christians along with Jewish converts. The name Tabeetha commemorates Peter's miracle of raising Tabitha or Dorcas from the dead, as written in the book of Acts.

Growing up in Palestine was a marvellous Biblical education. Living in the Garden Tomb was one thing, but David had already seen so much of the culture and places that feature in the stories of the Bible. The raven that dropped the coin on the dusty road in Jericho was no doubt related (in a very very distant way) to the ravens who fed Elijah 3000 years before. After all, Elijah's cave happened to be nearby!

Walking to church in Jerusalem was another exercise in Biblical education, as Uncle Politian explained the significance of the Via Dolorosa, the Temple area, the wailing wall, the Holy Sepulchre, the Damascus Gate, and other features of the city. If he didn't give geographical lessons, he would remind the children of what Jesus did in each part of the city.

All of this knowledge came in handy later on. When David expressed his shock at Australian children's lack of understanding of the Gospel events and Palestinian geography, at the age of 12, the Rector of Holy Trinity Wentworth Falls immediately gave him a Sunday School class to teach.

in sand with a gritty mouth and eyes a lot more than Lora did! But she wasn't averse to sand in its proper place, and they had some enjoyable times at Bet Yam beach. There were plenty of British people living in Jaffa at the time, one group of whom were Christians and Scripture Union enthusiasts. In late 1943 they celebrated Scripture Union's seventy-fifth anniversary with a bus trip out to the beach and their own beach mission, with choruses and a proper 'sand pulpit', followed by a party.

The warm months also brought another hospital trip for David, but this time it was not on the same level of seriousness as previously. David had got lightly sunburned, and a mass of little poxes appeared all over him. Lora, with her background of small-pox and its aftermath, was naturally alarmed, and the doctor put David into an ambulance (very exciting for a little boy) and whisked him off to the infectious diseases hospital. David didn't feel sick at all and enjoyed the luxury of having a great deal of attention and his own private room with a verandah overlooking the beach.

All the patients in nearby wards were British men, and some would come into his room to sit and talk, intrigued by this little boy. It was delightful for David to be treated for the first time in his life as an equal in thoughtful and satisfying conversation. One patient, who was suicidal, spent an hour with David every morning and afternoon, and finally decided that life was worth living.

Thankfully small-pox was never the diagnosis. The doctor decided that David had nothing more than sandfly bites on top of sunburn, and discharged him.

Jaffa was the location of David's first ever birthday celebration, at the age of seven. Lora went to a lot of trouble to find a few children to invite to a little party at the British swimming club. It would have been a dismal party by today's standards – David couldn't swim, and they had no cake or candles, but it was just for him and therefore special. This party was also the source of a great deal of confusion about his age, which was not cleared up for several years.

In the two years David had lived with the Politians he had celebrated his fifth and sixth birthdays on the same day as Mary's birthday, probably because it was easier for Aunty Politian. David worked on the logic that if Mary had a birthday, he had a birthday too. After he had moved out with Lora, at the age of six, Mary had invited him to her next birthday party, whereupon he naturally assumed that he was now seven.

The passing of a whole year between birthdays is a hard concept for most little children, and at the party Lora put on for him, he believed that he was now eight. He had no candles to blow out to clear up the confusion for him, and Lora never talked to him or to anyone else in his hearing about his age. So for the next ten years, David believed that he was a year older than he actually was.[5]

But all of these activities were not a regular part of day to day life. In the frequent times that David had nothing to do and no-one to play with, he would sit at the window of his bedroom, which was built onto the main street of Jaffa, and look out on the colourful bustle below.

There was a passing parade of characters at all times of the day and night: donkeys, nearly collapsing under impossibly heavy burdens, being beaten to keep them moving, goats and sheep being herded in flocks under the guardianship of young boys, buses bursting to the seams with travellers coming into town, army and police vehicles buzzing up and down. Watching the mental patients from the asylum across the road as they sat on the pavement also provided some entertainment.

A very common sight was a Muslim funeral procession; the Imam would walk in front, leading the chanting, and behind would come professional mourners, women who were paid to wail at

---

[5] This confusion was even carried on by Lora inadvertently. Before taking him back to Australia with her later on, she wrote an affidavit saying he was nine years old where in fact he was still only eight.

funerals. These women would collect their tears in olive wood bottles, and then bury the bottles with the body. At the tender age of seven, David was already so acquainted with death that these funeral processions seemed normal to him. Death was just part of life, like having three meals a day.

And happily, Lora and David were eating regularly now that they had some money. Their main diet was still flat, Arabic *pita* bread which could be stuffed with olives or dried fruit. David persuaded Lora that he was responsible enough to make the daily trip into the old part of Jaffa[6] to buy the bread. He had an ulterior motive: adventure! The excitement of exploring the rabbit warren of tiny streets and shops was only slightly surpassed by sitting for long periods watching the baker, or trying to talk to people in his now broken Arabic.

Lora came with him on Fridays to buy two eggs for Sunday. Some skill was needed in choosing the eggs. They had to be tested in a bucket of water; a fresh egg would sink, and a bad egg would float to the top. Boiled eggs on Sunday were a Claydon family tradition, as was a traditional cooked lunch after church. Unfortunately, Lora was still too poor to afford any meat apart from the occasional portion of camel or goat, so Sunday lunch for Lora and David was oranges fresh from the orange grove at Tabeetha's tomb.

Even with some friends, school lessons and trips into Jaffa, David still had many periods of loneliness and boredom. Lora would sometimes go up to Jerusalem for the day and he would have to amuse himself. He had no toys or games, and only one book - 'Little Black Sambo'.

Lora meant well, but she was not warm, nor particularly patient. She didn't seem to have the understanding of what was an age-

---

[6] The old part of Jaffa was run down, in a poor condition and off limits to some. Big signs said, "Out of Bounds to Defence Forces". Today the area has been restored and rebuilt and is a beautiful housing and shopping area.

appropriate activity for a bright, intelligent child with high spirits. Her own strict, Victorian upbringing gave her the idea that David, at the age of six or seven, should and could learn a Psalm by heart on cold wet winter days. If he had not learned the set passage by the end of the day, he was deemed to be 'naughty' by Lora and was punished severely.

Unwittingly Lora was building up a bank of resentment and bitter feelings in her young charge. She truly loved children and did have a real concern for David, but she did not understand him nor was she fair to him. This would be a cause of dissension between them for the rest of David's growing years.

CHAPTER FIVE

NOW FOR A HAPPY CHILDHOOD STORY

On the other side of the world, another child had been growing up, in completely different circumstances. With a stable, loving family, in the relative peace of war-time Sydney, Robyn Hickin was a child who in the years to come, was to experience no major difficulties and no substantial disruption to her life.

This happy little girl was born on November 13, 1935, to a vibrant Christian couple, Ronald and Madelon Hickin. Madelon was from a strong and talented Christian family, the Arrowsmiths, well known in evangelical Sydney circles. Her brother was Canon Bert Arrowsmith, a missionary in China, a prominent preacher in Sydney and later the Commonwealth Secretary of the Bible Society.

Ronald was converted at about the age of 19 when he and Madelon met at a tennis club. She brought him to the Church of Christ at Auburn, and he soon made a decision to become a Christian, and soon after married Madelon. From the beginning his faith was very firm, and, with a gift for writing, which he had honed as a boy writing (unpublished) Westerns, he very soon became a contributor to Christian journals.

Ronald was an accountant at the head office of Kolynos, a popular supplier of chemist goods, and the little family was living at Strathfield when Robyn was born.

Five years later, moving south to Bexley North, they discovered no local Anglican church in their suburb, so they started a small Christian meeting in the garage of the local taxi driver.

It can't have been easy, or roomy. Robyn has vivid memories of people of all ages tightly packed into the garage singing 'Now the Day is Over' at the conclusion of every evening service.

But Ronald and Madelon were committed to Christian ministry, and while he was working, Ronald was also studying theology in preparation for ordination in the Anglican church. He began plans for the building of a church, and, when it was completed, he became the first curate-in-charge of Holy Trinity, Bexley North.

The Hickins' ministry began and continued as a team ministry. Robyn's parents started the Sunday School, a youth group, a Girls' Friendly Society (GFS), a Boys' Brigade, a ladies' fellowship and a church choir trained by the musically talented Madelon.

Ronald was a thoughtful, biblical preacher with a good sense of humour. In later years, when writing to his children and grand children, he signed his name with a bald head with one hair sticking out of it and a clerical collar hovering under the chin.

Madelon, inheriting her family's gifts, was a talented, determined young woman, who had not been given all the educational opportunities she would have liked. But she had strong opinions and plenty of initiative, and found ways to use what she had, becoming a vibrant public speaker who was soon invited all over Sydney to speak at women's conferences and youth rallies.

In 1939, when Robyn was three, she became a big sister to Marlene and the little Hickin family was complete. The two little girls started out and continued as great friends, doing almost everything together. From a very early age, following the example of their parents, they became involved in the life of the church.

Robyn had drive and determination even as a baby. One photo taken on a trip to Manly at the age of about three, shows her striding ahead of the family, not taking the outstretched hand offered to her.

The day Robyn started kindergarten at Burwood public school, she lasted all of ten minutes before she climbed out of her classroom window and ran across the playground, hoping to find her mother still there.

"Mother," she said. "I've had enough of school. I'm ready to go home."

Luckily for Robyn, Madelon had equal amounts of determination and lovingly, but firmly, took her back to class.

Like all children of the era, Robyn's early years were affected by the war that was still raging around the world. Although there were no bombs, there were still precautions, and the air-raid siren rang out fairly often from the local butcher's shop. Robyn and her classmates took the warnings seriously and hid under the school desks, with cotton wool in their ears and pegs in their mouths, if needed, to stifle their screams. Everyone had to carry a small air-raid bag to school with things to block their ears if the bombs fell.

Thankfully, the Hickins were relatively untouched by the global tragedies which affected so many others, and Robyn and Marlene's family continued close-knit, warm and stable despite a few moves to come.

In 1945, when Robyn was 10, the family moved to Cammeray where Ronald became the rector of All Saints' Anglican church. Ronald initially may not have been terribly popular in the parish. He and Madelon had strong ideas about things that were 'not done' by Christians. These were the days when Christians definitely didn't dance, so he cancelled the weekly Saturday night dance in the hall within a month of arriving, much to the dismay of the locals. Robyn was unaffected by the consternation, and the age of 10 became a turning point for her in two ways. First, she became conscious of her choice to be a Christian.

Robyn had always thought of herself as a Christian and had known that she had loved Jesus from a very early age. It seemed natural; her parents were Christians, so she was too. But at the age of ten, after hearing her father preach about making a decision to follow Christ, Robyn felt she needed to be sure.

"Daddy, I think I was converted tonight." she said to Ronald.

"Do you believe that you belonged to Jesus from the very beginning?" he asked her gently.

"Of course," she said.

"I don't think you were converted tonight. I think you said, 'I want to affirm this for myself'," he replied.

The second turning point for Robyn came at school. Robyn and Marlene had started at Cammeray Public School, but Robyn was in sixth class, at the end of primary school, with high school just around the corner. The sense of the future approaching gave her a spark of ambition. She made a conscious decision to study hard so as to get into the highly regarded and selective North Sydney Girls' High.

There were many days sitting on the verandah after school and on weekends, reading text books and trying to remember the Australian rivers from the north right down the East coast of Australia, as well as dates, names and journeys of early Australian explorers.

Robyn was a bright little girl and the study paid off with a successful exam result. She began at North Sydney Girls in 1948. However, her career there was short-lived, as after only six months the Hickins were on the move again. This time Ronald became the rector of the historic stone church of St Paul's, Redfern.

Redfern was not what anyone would describe as an easy parish. Right in the heart of hard-up Sydney, St Paul's beautiful historic stone buildings seemed at odds with some of the residents who were homeless and destitute.

Some people seemed to live in the church grounds, and a few more resided on the Hickins' front porch. Robyn and Marlene would often have to step over people who had decided to go to sleep on the Rectory doorstep.

STATUTORY DECLARATION

I,   LORA CLAYDON

of "Verna" Main Western Highway Wentworth   in the State of New South Wales,
                                    Falls
Spinster   do solemnly and sincerely declare as follows:

1.   I am the Guardian of DAVID CLAYDON of Wentworth Falls aforesaid
Student.

2.   I became Guardian of the said David Claydon in the year One
thousand nine hundred and forty by virtue of an Order made by the
British Mandate in Palestine; prior to this date the said David Claydon
was cared for by the Bethlehem Babies Home. The said David Claydon was
baptised in the year 1940 and he was given my family name and named
David Claydon and from that time I have brought him up as my adopted
nephew.

3.   The said David Claydon had no Birth Certificate and his birth
date was determined by ex-ray of the wrist by a Medical Practitioner
in Jerusalem as approximately the 5th October, 1936.

4.   The then High Commissioner for Palestine, Sir M. MacMichael
issued a Passport to the said David Claydon after obtaining the necessary evidence for same from the said Bethlehem Babies Home and the
Palestine Government Welfare Officer.

5.   All records relating to David Claydon were destroyed when the
King David Hotel Jerusalem was blown up at the termination of the
British Mandate.

And I make this solemn declaration conscientiously believing the same to be true and by
virtue of the provisions of the "Oaths Act 1900."

Subscribed and declared at   Katoomba
this   18th   day of   February,   Lora Claydon.
one thousand nine hundred and fifty-three. four
before me   Rebecca J.P.

Lora Claydon's Statutory Declaration indicating guardianship status

Lora as a missionary in India with her friend Jiwan

David in a meditative mood, Cairo 1945

Lora with Tikitibu and David, 1940

*David and Robyn 1993 on rooftop of
Politian home where David played as a child*

Dr Cyril and Mrs Politian and Mary with David and Lora,1943

The Garden Tomb

Wardens House in the Garden Tomb grounds

David (far right), Captain of the Katoomba High School Debating team with team members: John Moore and Judith Jack with teacher, Harold Went, 1953.

Robyn and Marlene 1941

Robyn with Juvenile Jury team, 1947

Harry Huen, 1954

David in Cairo wearing his English Mission College jacket and his crusader badge, 1945

Hickin family at St Paul's Redfern, 1955

"Wingham" students with Dr R.R. Winton in front row right, 1956

Wedding with Robyn's parents and Lora, 1961

The Hickins faced constant requests for help from people in desperate circumstances. Instead of money, they offered food, and Madelon became famous among the homeless for her bulky salad sandwiches and mugs of hot tea.

Amazingly, this experience amongst down-and-outs did not seem either to worry or to place a burden of guilt on Robyn. She was never afraid of the local 'residents' at the church, but instead had great faith in what her parents were doing to try to help them.

The Hickins had always talked about their ministry around the kitchen table, and this continued in Redfern. Ronald and Madelon did not keep much from their daughters, expecting them to keep confidences and contribute to the discussion. Seeing their accepting attitude towards people who were in difficulties gave Robyn a similar belief that everyone should be treated with respect, not looked down on because of their circumstances.

But school was different altogether. Halfway across Sydney, and half a world away from the problems of Redfern and homeless destitutes is Meriden, a girls' Church of England school in well-to-do Strathfield. To help pay the fees, Madelon took a job singing and playing the organ at a local funeral home and enrolled Robyn and Marlene in Meriden. The girls caught the train every day from Redfern to Strathfield to continue their education.

While the train trips were enjoyable, Fridays were a special highlight. Lilian Arrowsmith, Madelon's sister, worked near Redfern station and would meet the girls in the morning with a block of chocolate for each of them. School rules required that the girls not eat on the train, so showing great restraint they kept their chocolate to eat and share on the weekend.

On Friday afternoons their parents met them at school and drove them home in their first and very newly acquired family car. Madelon can't have been too concerned about the upholstery because she always brought cakes and lemonade for the journey home.

Robyn's school days at Meriden were happy ones. She had many interests, good friends and a lot of energy. She played tennis, learned music, did debating, sang in the choir and acted in the school plays. Drama had been a special love from the time she was little.

Her marks were good, and even great when she worked hard, but her philosophy for most of high school was to not let study interfere with her life except when necessary! And life was good. Robyn faced no traumas, no obvious teenage crises, and no major self-doubts. The typically 'troubled' teen years might as well have been unknown for her. She got on well with her friends, and better with her parents. Life was simple and fun, and even her infractions were minor.

There were a few odd occasions when she did fall foul of the rules, but even these falls from grace and their accompanying punishments would be considered small today. As Meriden was a church school, once a term there was a communion service before school. It was compulsory for girls to bring their own prayer books, but, on one occasion, Robyn had forgotten to take her prayer book home the night before. On the morning of the service she had to climb over a verandah and go to her locker to retrieve it, well before the official school opening time. She wasn't caught, but she spent the whole of the service looking furtively at the staff, expecting to get into trouble!

In fact, lockers seemed to be her undoing. In sixth form, she should have had her book ready for her Divinity lesson, but again, she had forgotten it. The Divinity teacher was also the headmistress, and Robyn, like all the girls, was fairly apprehensive of her.

"I've probably just got time to get to my locker and get the book if I hurry," she thought, but it wasn't to be.

As she bent down over her locker she sensed the formidable figure of Miss Hannam towering over her. The punishment for not being ready in the classroom was to learn all the seasons of the church year by heart.

Miss Hannam may have been scary, but Robyn was not put off by a little fear from getting what she wanted. And what she wanted was to start a Crusader[1] group at school. Meriden was a Christian school, but, according to Miss Hannam, it didn't need anything other than chapel and Divinity lessons, so there was no Crusaders.

Robyn could see from other schools how useful Crusaders was to young Christians, and, as a keen believer, she wanted to encourage her friends in their faith and reach out to others, so every year from year eight on she summoned all her courage and went to the dreaded Miss Hannam's study.

Knock knock. "Excuse me, Miss Hannam," Robyn would say.

There would be a long pause. Miss Hannam always knew when a student was at the door, but would continue to write without looking up so the poor child would be left in suspense for some time.

"I was wondering if you would give me permission to start a Crusaders group at lunch times," Robyn would say confidently. "I think it would be a great thing to encourage the girls who are Christians."

Every year Robyn would ask the same question, and, although Miss Hannam always greeted her kindly, the answer was always the same.

"I'm afraid not," or "No, Robyn, you can't," or "Sorry, it's not possible."[2]

Despite the rebuffs, Robyn kept asking. The gifts of persistence and determination, as well as faith and Christian love, were growing in her. They would be gifts that would see her achieve many things for God in future years.

---

[1] Crusaders was a voluntary student group in a school, very similar to the Scripture Union Inter-School Christian Fellowship (ISCF).

[2] Marlene was braver than Robyn and started an informal prayer group anyway. Years later the two girls were delighted to learn that a Crusader group, which is still going strong, had started at Meriden when a new headmistress came.

In the meantime, this happy, contented, stable child had no idea that her future years would be entwined with the little boy whose life was so very different from her own, still half a world away.

CHAPTER SIX

FROM PALESTINE TO AUSTRALIA

The vivid, colourful days in Jaffa lasted only nine months, and, true to form, Lora was again on the move.

This time she found a job as an interpreter at the Royal Indian Base Hospital camp near Lydda.[1] Her fluency in Urdu and Hindi from her days in India was coming in useful again. She translated for British doctors and the 'Diversional Occupational and Social Service Worker' who were treating Indian servicemen, and thought up creative activities for the patients to keep their minds off their plight.

Strictly speaking, family members of defence force personnel were not allowed on the base, so David was given a job and an army battle jacket to justify his existence. He was the official English teacher to the non-commissioned officers who were guards at the camp! Lora gave him a program to follow and he spent an hour a day 'teaching' the soldiers. The results of his task were questionable: he probably learned more Hindi than they learned English. But at least he could stay on the base, and the rest of his days were free. He wandered around the wards talking to soldiers, many of whom were amputees, and who were still suffering phantom pains and itches in their non-existent limbs.

Lora was still trying to find a way for herself and David to leave Palestine. Because of the war, it was not as simple as buying a ticket to get on a ship; travel was restricted, and travel plans had to be kept secret for security reasons. Lora had been negotiating with the

---

[1] Lydda was later known as Lod. The airstrip in Lydda was made into the international airport a decade later. During the war many countries had hospital bases in this area as it was the closest safe place for major surgery, especially amputations.

government to repatriate them to Australia, and after a few months at the base, she was told to be on stand-by in Jerusalem, so that she would be ready to go to Egypt, and from there put on a ship to return home.

The soldiers gave them a farewell from the base in October 1944, and kindly included a birthday cake for David. He was turning eight, but he thought he was nine, and again, no-one bothered to correct him. This little boy wandering around amongst the soldiers must have charmed the Colonel of the base, because he gave him a birthday present of a leather photograph album from Egypt. David still has it to this day.

Of course, Lora and David still had to get from Lydda to Jerusalem. This also was not as simple as it sounded. The Lydda-Jerusalem road had become notoriously dangerous. Only a few weeks previously, the British High Commissioner and his wife were travelling in a convoy of military vehicles on the road with plenty of soldiers as protection, but were ambushed by Zionists dressed as Arabs, pretending to mend the road. Incredibly the High Commissioner and his wife escaped, but many soldiers, including his personal bodyguard and driver, were killed. Bodies were left in the scrub around the road. The wounded, who retreated to the caves on one side of the road, died for want of help. None of the bodies had been recovered for fear of reprisal attacks, and the stench of rotting flesh was horrifying.

An armed convoy escorted Lora and David, travelling in an army truck, on the tense hour-long journey through this danger and on to Jerusalem.

The Clarks, still at the bank and still in Jerusalem, were again good friends to Lora and David, and invited them to stay on their property. The Barclays Bank manager in those days enjoyed large grounds with a sweeping drive bordered with a hedge of lavender, a small forest with a herd of deer, a grass tennis court (employees were invited in to play on Saturdays) and a typical English garden complete with fish pond.

David had the run of the property, while Lora spent her days in town, presumably pursuing immigration matters with the government, but he soon became bored and lonely. The Clarks had no children, Mrs Clark was not particularly interested in him, and Mr Clark, who was friendlier, was at work all day. David tried to hang around the Palestinian servants' quarters, hoping that someone would stop and talk to him, but he was usually ignored.

Sometimes Lora stayed away for several days, so David would be invited to stay in the Clarks' own home. It was a novel experience for him to be bathed by the servants and sit at the large dining room table with a servant standing behind him to meet his every need.

The only respite from boredom at the Clarks' came if the staff were cleaning the fish pond for a baptism on Sunday. David was allowed to take his clothes off and have a small dip in the water. But one day some exciting news came in. The High Commissioner, who was leaving, had decided to have his farewell at the Clarks' property. This was a big event.

Security was tight because of the Lydda-Jerusalem road attack, and soldiers lined the road all the way from the High Commissioner's residence to the Clarks' property. Soldiers were behind every tree in the grounds, and all around the six foot perimeter stone wall. Even better than watching all the guards was tasting every tray of tasty morsels that caterers kept bringing in for the garden party. David was quite sick that night!

While daytime was relatively peaceful, nights were filled with Zionist bombings of government buildings. Bombings for David were very common and he was not usually scared. The barn-like house Lora and David were staying in would shudder with each blow, and, on their first night, the glass in their windows shattered. This was a new experience for David and it frightened him a little;

in all the other places they had stayed, the glass in the windows had long since disappeared, but the Clarks had thoughtfully replaced it for them before they came. Eventually, as in most places, all the glass was broken and they depended on wooden shutters for protection against the weather.

The Zionist planes were small and flew at a very low altitude, so air raid warnings and the blackout on windows and lights at night were not effective against them. Occasionally sirens would sound for a German plane, and everyone would go to an air raid shelter, but this was becoming less common. Eventually the government decided to lift the evening curfew and the night blackout, as the war in Europe was affecting Jerusalem less and less. To celebrate, bells were rung from the YMCA tower one evening, and Lora took David to see it and the King David Hotel. It was the first time in his life David had ever seen people on the street at night, let alone street lights and windows all lit up like fairyland.

Lora was always keen to worship with other Christians, and David went with her to Christ Church at Jaffa Gate on Sunday mornings. In the afternoons he went to the High Commissioner's residence[2] for a Crusaders' meeting. Sixty or so children would sit on the lawn overlooking the Jordan Valley singing Scripture Union choruses like 'Wide, wide as the Ocean' and 'Do you want a Pilot?' David's imagination often got the better of him and he would sit trying to imagine the Jordan Valley full of water, and himself piloting a boat across it. After singing the children were split up into classes. The Crusaders' method of memorizing Scripture was more reasonable than Lora's. Thirteen weeks of remembering one text a week earned David a Crusader badge.

Little David was having a thoroughly Christian upbringing. Never having a particular 'conversion' experience, he always called himself a Christian and unconsciously took on Lora's faith and

[2] This later became the United Nations Headquarters for the Israel-West Bank operation.

teaching for himself. Living in Jerusalem certainly helped matters; growing up, he knew that Jesus was a real person, who, like himself, had walked the streets of Jerusalem! He had seen the places where the miracles had all happened. Indeed, having experienced two miraculous healings himself, and having seen God's miraculous provision for himself and Lora in times of need, David had no trouble accepting the gospel stories as truth.

Finally, in November 1944 the 'stand-by' period in Jerusalem came to an end. Lora and David packed their few belongings and said their good-byes.

Unfortunately David's very few belongings were depleted even further when Lora made him give away his precious grey felt kangaroo.

David had been talking to his kangaroo every night to go to sleep for the four years since it had been given to him, but Lora thought that was long enough.

"There's another little child at Christ Church who needs a toy," she stated. "You're lucky to be going to Australia where you can see a real kangaroo!"

The kangaroo was given away: the child who received it seemed very pleased, but David cried until Lora made it clear that tears would not be tolerated.

Some comfort came from the rector of Christ Church, David's godfather, who visited them on their last evening in Jerusalem. He prayed for Lora and David on their long journey to Australia, and gave David a small New Testament. It wasn't a grey kangaroo, but it was a precious gift, and he kept it for the rest of his life.

Getting to Egypt was a hazardous experience. It was an overnight train trip from Jerusalem to Cairo, and trains were attacked regularly by Zionists. The British came up with a tactic to stop passenger trains being blown up: they would place some captured Zionist and Palestinian guerrillas in a cattle carriage and link it to the front of the engine. Goods trains were not generally as protected. Lora and David boarded their passenger train in Jerusalem. The train line was a single track, with some lay-bys. The train was delayed in departing, and, about half an hour out of Jerusalem, their train stopped. A goods train, carrying sheep and cattle coming towards Jerusalem, had hit a mine, and was in disarray. The encaged sheep were burning alive, and carriages were straggled down the steep mountainous incline.

The attack had happened at the by-line, and was probably meant to happen in such a way that it would have caused damage to Lora and David's passenger train without hurting the prisoners in the front cage. God's grace in slowing their train down was not unnoticed by Lora and David. They went on their way realizing that they could easily have been killed.

But the train did arrive in Cairo, and David woke in the morning to the raucous noise of porters bargaining with Lora and with each other to carry the luggage. In her limited Arabic Lora negotiated a price, and they piled into one open-top horse-drawn carriage, with their baggage following behind in another, heading for the YWCA.

David's education, which had been hit and miss up until this point, was broadened in Cairo by some sightseeing and visits to the Antiquities Museum, but he did go to school as well for a short time. Lora placed him with a missionary couple at Heliopolis, just outside Cairo, and sent him off to the nearby English Mission College[3]. Typically, Lora didn't tell David what she was doing or why she was gone, so he was left for a month with this family. But it wasn't a bad experience – just disruptive. He enjoyed school, especially playing marbles in the dusty courtyard, and he joined the Cubs briefly, playing on the Heliopolis sand hills.

---

[3] The College was in one of the palaces which the previous King Faud had for his wives. The king at the time, Farouk, only had one wife, so his father's palaces were used for other purposes. The College still existed in 1980 when David returned for a visit, but the sand hills of Heliopolis had changed greatly, and were now covered in apartment buildings.

Lora came to get David for Christmas, and they visited English CMS missionaries at the Harpur Memorial Hospital in Menouf, on the Nile Delta.[4] But they were soon on the move again, this time to Port Suez, where they were to wait for a ship. Lora taught briefly at a Christian school, but it was a rushed and uncertain stop. Finally they were given only 12 hours notice to front up at the docks to be put on board a ship for Australia.

Nothing on this trip was going to be simple. When Lora and David turned up with their luggage, ready to go, they faced some tough questioning from Immigration officials about David's legal status. Lora's own papers were in order, but as David had never had a proper birth certificate, his documents were slightly unusual. Lora was a tough customer when she wanted to be, and she wasn't about to leave David behind. She stood her ground and argued fiercely that not only did his passport show David to have the Claydon name, but she had a legal document declaring her to be his guardian. Thankfully the officials didn't question too hard, or they may have discovered that Lora's legal document was not a court order, but only her own affidavit!

Finally immigration was over, and Lora and David were taken out with two others in a motor boat to the middle of the harbour where a cargo and passenger ship, the 'Umtata', was waiting. Everyone had to climb the rope steps up the side of the ship. For little David, who was carrying a few bags as well, the distance between steps seemed so great that he thought would fall between them into the water.

The 24 passengers sharing 12 cabins were all senior Australian or New Zealand army officers. David, Lora and another lady with a daughter were the only civilians on board. The *Umtata* was quite a

---

[4] Christmas is based on the Coptic word meaning 'to be born' so it was an interesting experience to spend one Christmas in Egypt where the word has its roots. David enjoyed exploring Menouf's canals and muddy streets after the December rains.

small ship which had been commandeered from the South African merchant navy. Apart from the soldiers, army trucks and other armed forces gear, the cargo was mostly gum-arabic, used for making glue, ink and medicine. This was highly inflammable, as the captain explained very seriously to his new passengers.

"If we are attacked by the enemy, German or Japanese, we will explode, so there is no point in doing life-boat drill," he said, going through the details of the various warning systems.

"If a plane attacks us, the alarm will be short bursts. Go below decks to the dining saloon. If a submarine attacks us it will be long blasts. Come in here to the lounge. Officers are to work out among themselves a roster to man the four anti-aircraft guns, and the anti-submarine depth charges."

Despite the warnings, the trip down the Red Sea was calm and uneventful, and they were able to spend at day at Aden's port. David watched Africans carrying bags of coal on their shoulders into ships' holds, supervised by Arab masters. The workers may have been paid, but it would not have been enough money to put up with the verbal abuse coming from the Arabs. It was like slave labour!

Many ships in the war travelled in convoy, but the *Umtata* was going to be on its own. After it entered the Indian Ocean, it zig-zagged on its long voyage until it reached the north-west coast of Australia.

In the frequent long periods that David had spent out of formal schooling, Lora never supervised him in doing any schoolwork from home. So David broadened his own education: he talked to the officers, learning how the anti-aircraft guns and the depth charge mines worked, learning rope knots, the marine flag alphabet and the whole range of ranks in the three defence forces. He also taught himself how to type, sitting on the deck with Lora's small portable typewriter and a touch-typing instruction card.

The ship reached Fremantle after three and a half weeks. The most dangerous part of the voyage had proceeded without incident, but things were still not smooth sailing. For some reason, no-one was allowed ashore. Some of the passengers weren't happy about this; a Lieutenant Colonel spat on the wharf saying, "If they won't allow me to touch the ground, I'll give them a little of myself", and the *Umtata* was required to sail across the Bight to Melbourne before anyone could disembark.

They sailed on, but as they started to cross the Great Australian Bight, they were warned of a German long range U-boat submarine which had already sunk 14 coastal ships, three in the immediate area. The Australian navy had one ship out looking for it, and it was thought to be heading in the direction of the *Umtata*. It was evening when the Captain announced this to his passengers in the lounge.

The whole group decided to stay up and pray all night for safety, apart from those on the guns and depth charges roster. David was deemed too young for all of this and was sent protesting to bed.

"Totally unfair," he thought, but he quickly fell into the wonderful sleep of the innocent and unconcerned, and woke the next morning to ask desperately what had happened – clearly the ship was still there, and they were all not dead.

The news came at a bleary-eyed breakfast that the U-boat had in fact been very close to them, and had posed a great risk to them the day before they had found out about it! A large cargo ship a day behind the *Umtata* had been the bait which had drawn the U-boat away. Thankfully the U-boat had been found some days later and sunk off the coast of Western Australia. Everyone said prayers of thanks, and went to bed for a well-earned rest.

The event was momentous for all the passengers, but even more so for David. He was becoming extremely aware of God's protection on his life. Not only had he miraculously survived several serious illnesses, he had been rescued from the orphanage, had been provided for, and had been kept safe on many hazardous legs of this journey to Australia. David had a moment of clear realization that God had kept him for a purpose.

"I've obviously been kept alive for a reason," he thought to himself. "And I've ended up in Australia, which seems to be better than England or India, so God must want me to do something for him."

At the tender age of eight, he promised God that when he grew up, he would serve him in some form of full-time ministry for the rest of his life. It was a promise that would be fulfilled more quickly than he thought, and it was a promise that God would honour greatly.

So it was with this purpose in life, and faith in God, that David finally arrived with Lora, in Melbourne, Australia, on 3 March 1945.

Chapter Seven

Don't settle in too soon: you'll have to change again!

Lora and David had arrived in Melbourne, complete with numerous small parcels which contained all their worldly possessions, ready to start their new life in Australia.

It was not an auspicious beginning. Lora had not organised anything; as usual she was content just to see what would happen next, so she and David picked up all their little pieces of luggage and went to the YWCA for two nights. Then she decided it would be best to take the train to Sydney, so again, they picked up all their luggage and went off to the station.

The Sydney trip involved taking an evening train to Albury, and then standing on the station, waiting for the Sydney train to arrive.[1] The train was an all nighter. Lora and David sat up on a bench seat in second class, surrounded by all the parcels they were carrying. Lora's philosophy on luggage was to pack in small enough bags so that she could carry everything herself. It worked well – in theory. But from David's perspective, she always seemed to be carrying hundreds of bags and he had to carry a lot of them.[2]

Thankfully, when they reached Sydney's Central Station, they left the offending luggage at the baggage counter and travelled on the suburban line to Wahroonga, on Sydney's north shore. This was where two of Lora's sisters were now living, following the death of both of their parents. David and Lora walked to 16 Bundarra Ave and rang the door bell.

---

[1] The Victorian rail gauge was wider than the NSW rail gauge.

[2] In reaction to this, in years to come, David developed his own packing skills so that he could travel around the world carrying nothing more than an overnight bag and a camera. Occasionally he would psyche himself up to carry home an extra suitcase for a missionary.

"I'm just on the phone," came a lady's voice. "I won't be long!"

"That's my older sister Freda," said Lora to David.

"Does she know we are coming?" asked David to Lora.

"Oh no, we aren't allowed to tell anybody about travel plans when there is a war on," said Lora.

David inwardly rolled his eyes. "Oh no," he thought to himself. "This is typical. This poor old sister is about to have a heart attack."

It had been a good 11 years since Lora had left Australia, and Freda hadn't seen her in all this time. When she finally came to the door, she looked, gasped, and said, "Just a minute – I'm on the phone!"

Then she went back to the phone, leaving David and Lora standing at the door, and explained to the person on the other end of the phone that there was someone at the door, and she would have to go.

"Why didn't she say that her sister is at the door?" whispered Lora to David under her breath.

But David didn't reply with what he was thinking: "Who would want to admit to having a sister who just appears out of the blue!"

Poor Freda finally got over her shock and let them in. She was slightly more shocked and swallowed hard when she realised that Lora expected her to put them up for a while. For a start, she and Lora would have clashed because she was an extremely organised person with a strict daily routine. However, the real issue was more about David.

Freda was quite embarrassed at having a single sister with a child. Even though she knew that David had been found in the orphanage, and had no biological connection to Lora at all, he was white, and Lora was white, and people would draw their own conclusions, no matter how many times Freda told the story.[3]

---

[3] In previous years Freda had looked after a little Fijian boy for some time, but she would have considered their different appearances enough evidence to stop innuendo and rumours.

Lora herself didn't seem to be too concerned about people's perceptions of her and David, even though she was aware of it. But she was always clear in stating that David was her *nephew*, or *adopted* nephew, when she needed to say something. In fact, this was not strictly true, and the legal issues of the adoption came up again when they arrived in Australia.

Lora was David's guardian, but she had no legal rights to call herself his aunt. Thinking he might like things formalised, she asked him if he wanted to go to court and become her real nephew. David's adamant refusal probably surprised and disappointed her, but he liked his status the way it was.

From his perspective, his parents were dead, and no-one else had the right to stand in for them. He understood that it was Lora's choice to look after him, and he happily called her 'Aunty', but he would never let her slip into regarding him as an adopted son. In fact, if anyone ever tried to 'mother' him, he ignored them outright and distanced himself from them.

As it was, living with Freda was not an option, and Lora would have to find somewhere else to stay.

The lower Blue Mountains, just out to the west of Sydney, were to be the location of choice for Lora. She had spent some years growing up in the area, and in her periods of stress illness as a missionary had recuperated there a number of times. The Claydon family had a house 'Verna' in Wentworth Falls. This wasn't available, but after a short stay in the property of a friend, Lora and David moved in temporarily with the lady who lived next door to 'Verna'.

It was a little house, with no bedroom for David, so Lora bought an old motor home for him to sleep in and parked it in the grounds. As Lora couldn't drive David never knew how she got it there!

By the middle of the year, at the age of eight, David was ready to start school again. So far in his life he had attended school for the total period of about one year. Even though he had taught himself facts from Arthur Mee's Children's Encyclopaedia, and had a broader range of knowledge and experience than most Australian children his age, he found fitting in to the combined years 3 and 4 class fairly difficult.

Not only was the syllabus hard to understand, but David risked social rejection because of his English accent and different experiences from his peers. He found the worlds of the Australian children very small and their horizons limited, compared to the children he had played with in Palestine and Egypt.[4]

In his second week at school, his teacher allowed him to speak to the class about where he had come from. The class laughed uproariously when he said, "the bus drivers in Palestine and Egypt spend more time under the bus than in it!" and he felt the glow of being able to share his experiences, and the relief of acceptance from the children around him.

Other children remembered him as being friendly, if quiet[5] as well as a little bit naughty. His boyish spirits were still not tamed. Miss Bell, the teacher, was sometimes exasperated with him, and sent him to the head teacher a few times for a caning.

David had strong opinions about this form of punishment.

"How stupid to think that a caning would change my attitude or my behaviour," he thought to himself the first time it happened.

---

[4] Studies of 'Third Culture Kids' or TCKs (children who have grown up in a culture different from that of their parents or guardians) in recent years have commented on this slight sense of superiority felt by TCKs because of their broader experiences

[5] Studies of TCKs have also commented on their methods of relating to their peer groups: Dr Ruth Useem wrote in one such study: "On the surface, most adult TCKs conform to what is going on around them in such a way that attention is not drawn to them. As they meet new people and situations, they are slow to commit themselves until they have observed what is expected. If what is expected is unacceptable or incomprehensible, they will quietly withdraw rather than make fools of themselves or hurt the feelings of others. Their bland and unremarkable exteriors, however, belie not only depths of feelings, but also considerable talents and a wealth of memories of other countries and places, including the expatriate communities in which they have lived abroad and continue to take an interest in."

The second time, he decided not to bother the head teacher, and hung around the corridor for an appropriate amount of time before returning to class quietly. He guessed correctly that Miss Bell had other things to do besides check that he had turned up for his caning.

While he needed to fit into the local scene, David still wanted to hang onto his past. On the walk to school every day he would revise his Arabic numbers and significant words that he still knew. Every week he seemed to lose another word, until finally he could only remember the numbers. Even these he forgot how to pronounce over the next few years, though he never lost how to write them. It was a sad slipping away of his mother tongue.

But things were about to change again for him. After only half a year at Wentworth Falls Primary, Lora decided, in consultation with Freda and another sister, Erna, that David should have a 'proper' education.

Dorothy Orton, an English friend and missionary colleague of Lora's from her days in India, had heard of David's existence and had left Lora £4,000 in her will so she could look after him.

For the first time in a long time, money was on tap, and, in 1946, Lora enrolled David as a boarder at Knox Preparatory School in Wahroonga. Again, there was a mix up about his age. Lora told the headmaster that David was 10, and thought he should have gone into year 5, but the school put him into year 4 because of his lack of schooling. It was probably the best decision because he was actually still only nine. However, his natural academic abilities started to show up when he did very well, coming second in the year, and he was advanced two classes the next year, going from year 4 to year 6.

Knox seemed more to David's taste than the local primary at Wentworth Falls. The boys mostly seemed more aware of the world and able to take on new experiences. He made friends quickly with brothers Tony and Edwin York, and spent every free Saturday and free weekends with them or another friend, Malcolm Gibb. The housemaster, Mr Knight, had served in the war and had some empathy and understanding for David's orphan status.

Making friends gave David the confidence to begin to use his natural gifts of leadership. About halfway through the year he had begun to share some of his experiences, and the way he had seen God work in his life, with Tony, Malcolm and some other boys. He suggested to them that, because God was so real in life, they should meet together every Sunday afternoon just to talk about God. Without even knowing about ISCF groups[6] David managed to begin one, lead it and sustain it at the age of nine, without any help from teachers.

Knox taught David some valuable lessons which he kept all his life. One of these was learning how to protest and confront calmly to get results.

In the past few years, there had been many occasions when David had been unjustly punished by Lora. His inability to learn Psalms on rainy days was just one example of this. Another case was when they were staying with the Clarks in Jerusalem. Mr Clark said that there was a tennis ball missing and Lora must have assumed that David had stolen it. He proclaimed his innocence, but Lora didn't choose to believe him and punished him severely for telling a lie.

Like most children, David had a strong sense of justice, and, when he was treated unfairly, he needed a way to express his own frustration. Up until now, he had sulked around after an episode of injustice. But this was to change.

For some reason, one day as the headmaster, Mr Quince, was passing David on the stairs, he said to him, "David you're a good boy. But you have one problem – you sulk when you are scolded."

---

[6] ISCF was the Inter-School Christian Fellowship, a movement of Scripture Union, which supported and nurtured Christian groups in Australian public schools.

The reproof played in David's head, so the next time he was treated unjustly he took another tack.

Mr Quince's son was a university student, and had been teaching at Knox for about a month for experience. Something happened to him (David never knew what) to make him extremely annoyed, and he was determined to find a culprit. None of the boys would own up to the evil deed, so the next day, Quince Jnr announced the names of three boys he had decided were responsible. To David's astonishment, his name was on the list. The boys were summoned to a classroom for three hard whacks of the cane, and were given no details of the crime they were supposed to have committed, nor any opportunity to plead their case.

"Aren't you going to cry like the other boys?" asked Quince Jnr surprised, when he saw David's eyes were dry. Not crying was the first form of protest for David, and he left the room, saying nothing.

But he had a plan. The three boys were boarders, so that night, David took the others with him and went in their pyjamas to the Headmaster's study to calmly tell their story. Mr Quince senior apologised, investigated the matter, and the boys never saw his son in the classroom again.

Meanwhile, back in the Blue Mountains, Lora was changing her plans again. She decided she needed somewhere permanent to live, so she used Dorothy Orton's money to build a fibro-cement house at Wentworth Falls. The money had originally been left to her for David's support, and she obviously thought that building a house fell into that category. Unfortunately building and landscaping 'Galilee' cost £2,500, and, by the end of David's first year at Knox, it was clear that there wouldn't be funds to keep him there.

Lora announced to the school at the end of the year that, even though he had done extremely well in his studies, she would have to withdraw him. The school announced back to her that, according to their rules, she had to give a term's notice, so David would have to stay. Stay he did, for the first term of the next year, but Lora still couldn't afford to keep him there and sent him back to Wentworth Falls primary.

It was a hard term for David. In a composite year 5/6 class the schoolwork seemed to have no connection with what the boys had been doing at Knox, and he just didn't get it. The new house was also further away from the school, and he had to trek two kilometres there and back every day. The only bright spot in the day seemed to be stopping at the corner of the Highway and Falls Road. Steel pipes just there were a great enticement for the local children to swing on, often dropping coins out of their pockets. David's well-practised eye for coins on the ground kept him supplied with the occasional sustaining ice block on his way home.

But Lora could see that he wasn't happy, and took advice from a couple holidaying in Wentworth Falls, who said David should go to the private school in Springwood, Blue Mountains Grammar School.

It was the third school in one year for David, but it was a better option for him than Wentworth Falls. He travelled by train every day for the rest of the year, but, in his first year of high school, in 1948, he moved into boarding. Almost all the boys there had fathers who had been killed or seriously wounded in the war (Legacy was paying their fees) so David felt he had something in common with them. The whole group of about 28 boys in his dorm were good friends, and he enjoyed the company.

But from an educational standpoint, the school left a lot to be desired. All the boys from year 6 in primary to fifth form in high school were divided into only three classes. David found it all too slow for his quick brain, so he and his desk mate, Max, had to find other ways to amuse themselves. As the school was right by the railway line, they played trains with their pens and kept an accurate record of every type of steam engine which passed by in the day.

The happy days of boarding lasted during term time, but in the holidays David had to return to 'Galilee' and to Lora, who was running out of money again.

To solve her problems this time she found a job as a nursing aid working night shift at a TB sanatorium, and sent David out to work for a market gardener in Leura. It was a small, but enjoyable operation; just David, the boss and another man. Some days of work were simply weeding the gardens, but other days involved driving the old 1936 Bedford truck door to door selling fruit and vegetables. David learned how to drive the truck, but he couldn't use the hand-crank to start it, so if he stalled the engine the boss would get annoyed, and have to get out and crank it himself.

David's first job netted him ninepence an hour, plus lunch, and sixpence for his bus fare. He handed all this much-needed money over to Lora when he got home.

But by the end of the year, she still was not managing financially and had to withdraw David from boarding. He still went to the Blue Mountains Grammar School, but as a day boy again, and now he took on an afternoon job as well – working in Campbell and Ross Bradford's Chemist shop at the bottom of Katoomba Street. The money was better than at the market garden - at one shilling an hour, but the travel and long hours took their toll.

Every afternoon, after school, David would catch the train up to Katoomba for work until the shop closed at 6pm, and then get the train home again. Night falls quickly in the winter months, and David was frequently scared as he walked home from the station. After so many years of ambivalence towards death as a child, the fear of war now seemed to have caught up with him. Knowing how so many people in Palestine were shot from behind, he could hardly cope with the sound of footsteps behind him, let alone walking through bush areas with moving shadows.

One cold evening, at the age of 12, as he walked off the Wentworth Falls railway station, a new taxi driver in the area offered to drive David home with a passenger she had already picked up. David assumed that this was a kind offer of a free ride, and gladly accepted, but was dismayed when he realised the taxi driver was expecting some money.

"That's two shillings, thanks," she said, as they got near home.

"I didn't realise it would be that much," said David. "I'm sorry – I don't have any money on me."

Neither the driver nor the other passenger offered to help him out of his predicament, so David had to agree to pay his fare the next day. This put him in quite a spot. He could hardly tell Lora of the problem; she demanded he give her all his wages, and she was short of money anyway. He did have exactly the right amount already saved for the offertory plate at church on Sunday, so he took that and paid the taxi driver. But he wanted to make up the money he had already promised to God.

The solution came from soft drink bottles! Over the next two weeks, he kept a look out for empty soft drink bottles, which were often discarded in a garbage area that he walked past on the way to school. He picked up any that he found and took them to be redeemed for twopence. Twelve bottles later, his two shillings were in the church plate.

After one term with David as a day boy at the Grammar School, Lora was still not managing to make ends meet, even with David's wages helping to pay the bills. She decided, yet again, to pull David out of school and enrol him in a public school. However, yet again, she forgot the need for one term's notice, so David was allowed to stay for a few weeks more before he enrolled in Katoomba High School in third term of second form in High School.

He was only 13 years old, but already in his life he had changed schools seven times, and lived in 16 different situations. And things were not about to get any easier.

CHAPTER EIGHT

BOYS AREN'T SUPPOSED TO CRY

At the age of 12, David had two important things happen to him. One of these wouldn't affect him until later, but the other would keep him grounded for the difficult teenage years approaching.

The first thing was a pain in the chest which was bad enough to send him to his local doctor.

"Unfortunately you have a heart murmur," explained the doctor. "It may be serious."

It was to turn out to be serious, but at the age of 12, who is overly concerned about such things? For the moment he stopped playing football at school and became a line umpire instead, but kept living normally.

The second important thing was his Confirmation. David had been baptised as a little boy in Jerusalem, when Lora first rescued him from the hospital and the orphanage. Since then, his knowledge of God and his faith had grown in ways we wouldn't normally think possible for a little child.

He had grown up believing himself to be a Christian; he knew that Jesus was a real person and had done real things; and, most importantly, he believed that he, David, had been saved from death many times for a purpose. He had already made the momentous decision to serve God for the rest of his life.

Confirmation was his chance to formalise all of this, and to rededicate his life to God publicly.

It was an important day for David but also for Lora, because the confirmation took place at Christ Church, Springwood, where Lora's father had been the much-loved rector 40 years before. Lora's and David's connection was cemented in a special way: they both loved the same God; they were both dedicated to his service; and they now both shared an affection for the same church.

It was just as well that they had something positive to build their relationship on, as things were going to get harder and harder between them.

The first minor disappointment for David came from the new school. He had learned so little at the Grammar School that he was once again behind for his class when he started at Katoomba High School. Third term in second year was a real struggle, and when he came to the new year, he found he would have to repeat.

Home life was also becoming more difficult. David was 13 and attending school, but also working late every afternoon. He ate dinner with Lora, but she would then leave to go to her night shift job at the TB Sanitorium.

Weekends offered no rest; Lora had revived her 'Graphic Way' enterprise to earn more money – each set earned £5 - but it was still just as much hard work. Most of David's weekends were spent cutting out 12 different skylines and 40 different characters and animals.

The constant activity and lack of rest were hard to take. Living with Lora was lonely as she was hardly ever there. As well, her tendency to give away David's few and meagre possessions was continuing. A few times, he came home from school to find that his books had disappeared off the shelf. Her pattern of doling out harsh punishments for minor bouts of 'naughtiness' had also not changed.

After a few months David had had enough.

He decided that if Lora wanted to treat him harshly for any more perceived misdeeds, he would refuse to allow her to touch him. This might have been good for him, but Lora didn't take it too well. She was infuriated with David. The tension in the house was thick and their relationship was strained.

By the time they had been living together for eight months, Lora realised that both of them would probably cope better apart, and she arranged for him to board at the BCA Hostel[1] in Wentworth Falls.

This was a good solution. David was happy amongst the 20 or so boys around his own age, and was under the supervision of good wardens. They had a wide range of organised activities and were well-occupied. Finally he felt more at peace in his surroundings.

And school started to be easier too. Repeating the year had actually been useful. He was making more friends, although he was still quiet and kept to himself a little.[2] He was also getting on top of the subjects. Public speaking was starting to become recognised as one of his talents, and he joined the debating team, but he was also reprising his role as school ISCF leader! This little Christian group was helped a bit by a teacher, but David took on planning the meetings, and giving talks or arranging for speakers to visit. Sometimes he was able to borrow Christian films to show to the group.

Lora felt it was a good solution for her too. Now relatively free of restraints, she was feeling the old itch to be on the move again. India had never been far from her mind, and after a few months she decided to uproot and go back. She left her teenage charge in Australia, supposedly in a secure and happy situation, doing fine at school.

But good solutions never seemed to last long enough. At the end of two years at the hostel, it was closed down and sold off. All the boys had to move out. Lora was still overseas, and once again, at the age of 15, David was without a place to stay, without real means to live and without a significant adult who had his best interests at heart.

---

[1] The Bush Church Aid Society, an Anglican organisation, ran hostels for country children, where they could live near to a high school.
[2] According to Bob Sutton, 2005.

Survival was becoming one of David's talents – and one of God's gifts to him. The beginning of his fourth year at high school saw him in this situation: he found accommodation in a hut at the back of a Christian guest house in Katoomba Street. The rent from 'Galilee' was £5 a week. This paid for his accommodation and food, which was £4/10/0 a week as long as he worked every evening, waiting on the table and washing up after dinner at the guesthouse. His good results at school had paid off as well; he won a bursary for fourth and fifth year high school for £1 per week, which just about covered his expenses. But there were no extras, and things were tight. By working whole weekends for the guesthouse, he earned enough to eventually buy himself a second hand bicycle.

On some weekends he hitchhiked down to Wentworth Falls to see Lora's aunt and uncle, who were living in the old family home 'Verna'. The Bauers were childless and generous, always giving David 10 shillings "for the bus fare", and warming not only his heart but his pocket as well. But this friendship was not to last long. By winter their health was so bad that they were moved to the Petersham Home of Peace. David was once again without any family contact at all, and it was beginning to affect him deeply.

By the end of David's Year 4 at Katoomba High, Lora had been away for more than a year, and David had to spend his summer holidays at the guesthouse. It wasn't really a holiday. On evenings and weekends he worked in the guesthouse, while during the day he found a job at Hawkes' hardware store, opposite the Katoomba railway station. The only thing that could have remotely resembled a holiday was the fact that he was camping! The guest house was full and David had to move out of his room to make way for people who could pay. His bedroom was now a tent pitched on the back lawn.

The constant activity, the workload and the loneliness were adding up until finally David could not cope any more. The Bartrops, the owners of the guest house, were having relatives to stay, and one night David saw Mrs Bartrop tenderly kiss her niece on the cheek. It was enough. David ran to his tent and cried bitterly for an hour. It was the beginning of a flood of tears which would engulf his final year at school. At the guest house he cried privately almost every night. For the first time, he truly felt the pain of being alone in the world.

What did it feel like, he wondered, to live as most of the young people did in his class at school, with parents who loved you? What was it like to have something simple like a real home with a carpet on the floor, on which you could just lie down and read whenever you wanted? How would it be to spend weekends with your family, or your friends, and not have to work days and nights to make ends meet?

Pain and raw emotion had set in, and it was not about to get any better, even though Lora had reappeared from India for the beginning of David's fifth year at high school. The Bauers had moved out of 'Verna' so Lora sold 'Galilee' and moved into Verna with David. This was to be the base for David's final year of schooling.

Even though David didn't always get on with Lora, at least she was somebody to talk to, they had something in common, and he knew she cared about him. It was the closest he was ever going to get to a real home. But by the end of first term, Lora was hardly ever there. What was she doing? She never told David, but she seemed to be in the city the whole week, and often on weekends as well.

David would arrive home from school to an empty house. When he felt like eating, he would light the wood stove so that he could warm up whatever bottled food was in the house. Often he couldn't be bothered and so ate it cold.

The loneliness was searing, and David found himself crying most evenings. For some respite, he would walk down to the Wentworth Falls railways station, sit in front of the blazing coal fire in the waiting room and wait for the 8.30pm train in the hope that Lora would be aboard. If she wasn't on it, he waited a whole hour for the last train of the night, the 9.30pm. Sometimes she was on it, but sometimes she wasn't. There were many nights when she just didn't come home.

One evening when Lora was home, David still couldn't stop crying when he went to bed. Imagine a matter-of-fact white-haired middle-aged spinster trying to comfort a weeping, inconsolable 16 year old boy.

"What are you crying about? Why are you so upset?" she asked, not able to understand where this burst of emotion had come from.

"I'm worried about my studies," was the only answer David could give her.

How could he say to her that he was ground down by the loneliness, by having to get his own meals, by being on his own night after night?

"I do so want to tell her the truth, but I just can't," he thought to himself.

But in a way, his answer was the truth. The energy he was expending in crying night after night was exhausting him. He could only just manage his basic homework. There was nothing left for extra study for his important final exams.

David desperately needed some human love and comfort, and God provided for him once again. Lora was often invited to share about her missionary experiences at different churches, and at Easter that year she spoke at church services at St Stephen's, Penrith.

A church family took on the task of entertaining Lora and David for meals on that day, and David immediately clicked with them. Rex and Bruce Upton were twins about six months younger than he was, and had lost their father to a heart attack when they were about five, so the three boys had something in common. Their mother, Gwen, was a kind, generous woman, who immediately saw David's need for company and invited him to spend weekends with them.

It was a friendship that was to last a lifetime. Every Saturday morning David would hitchhike the 25 kilometres to their house, and catch the train back to school on Monday mornings. The Uptons' home was a happy place, and the boys and their mother had fun together. Not too long had passed before Mrs Upton came to see David as her third son, and the family relationship continued for the rest of their lives.

It was a friendship that would just about save David's sanity as well. By October, Lora had decided to go back to India again, using the money from selling 'Galilee' a few months before. David was on his own again. Placed with an austere Brethren family with three younger children, he was now living in the empty Lutanda Home. David slept in the boys' dormitory end of the large, cold house, while his host family had the girls' end. Still, at least in his new quarters he was getting proper meals, even if there was no love.

But exams were drawing near, and young people need both good nutrition and warm affection to do well. David was in no condition to study. The tears were not going away. Whenever he went to his room, he cried and couldn't stop. He cried solidly for the entire exam period - two weeks of exams and one week off to study. The only relief came from weekends at the Uptons, but from Monday to Friday, whenever he went to his room, he began to cry again. After an hour or so, David would try to stop the tears, but all he could do was go to the little reed organ in a separate room and play hymns to comfort himself.

"I know that God at least loves me. I know Jesus is real. I know Jesus is alive," he said to himself over and over, trying to stop the tears.

"At least God loves me. I know Jesus is real. I know Jesus is alive. I know I'm never alone"

CHAPTER NINE

THE BEGINNING OF REAL LIFE

The Leaving Certificate, at the end of high school, was not the high point of David's academic career.

The tears and emotional energy that had drained from him left him little time or strength to study, and his results were not as good as he would have liked.[1]

Thankfully, the government was generous, and awarded him a scholarship to Sydney University.[2] With the future in his sights, David left the cold, lonely atmosphere of the Blue Mountains the instant his exams were over, and headed down to Sydney – the big smoke.

He had a purpose in mind: earn some cash to buy some clothes for uni! Money had been so tight in the past few years, and teenagers grow so fast, that the only clothes he now owned, given by a woman whose husband had died, didn't fit properly.

Finding work never seemed to be a problem for David. His new job over the summer was as an internal messenger boy in Drug Houses of Australia, in the heart of Sydney city. David worked all the overtime he could get, both to earn as much as possible, but also to keep out of the Anglican hostel he was boarding at in Petersham.

Once again, he had not found good digs. It might have been a Christian hostel, but the warden functioned more like a prison

---

[1] David always believed he would have done better in his Leaving Certificate if he had had better teachers. At the time he didn't think much of them. His Geography teacher taught them well about American economic geography but unfortunately the exam was entirely on physical geography! His English and Maths teachers were 'utterly hopeless', and when he discovered in later years how his wife Robyn taught English it confirmed what he had thought.

[2] There would have been very little chance that David could have gone to university without this scholarship. In those days students had to pay fees, and David could only just manage to meet his daily expenses with a few part-time jobs as it was.

warden. The young men staying there were rough, 'true blue' ocker blokes – not the sort of people that David had ever been successful in relating to. If David had to stay there, he couldn't see much joy to come from university life.

An answer was to come, but from an unlikely quarter. Lora came back from India in the January. And with her came a solution that would set David on the course of the rest of his life and provide him with stability, security and significance.

When Lora came back, having left David unhappy in the Blue Mountains, she found him unhappy this time in Sydney. He told her what he thought of the hostel, which wasn't a lot. But Lora had a number of contacts, and a lot of persuasion. She took David to see the General Secretary of CMS in New South Wales, Rev Clive Kerle, and presented the problem to him. Clive Kerle talked to David, found out his trouble and phoned Dr Ron Winton, the warden of the Anglican Hostel for Overseas Students, usually known as 'Wingham'. David went straight out to Drummoyne to meet Dr Winton, and was admitted to Wingham on the spot.

Wingham was the perfect place to live. The view was great for a start. The hostel sat on the waterfront at Drummoyne, looking directly at the Sydney Harbour Bridge, and the hostel's 'VS' sailing boat was available to take out on to the water. The facilities at Wingham were also good, with common lounge areas and small but comfortable shared bedrooms. But the company was the best part of being at Wingham.

He became one of 28 young men, mostly from East Asia, living under the calm, godly and wise guardianship of Dr Winton[3]. As few of the students had family in Australia, or could afford to return home in holidays, Wingham became their home, and the Wingham boys their family.

---

[3] Dr Winton was the Assistant Editor of the Australian Medical Journal at the time, as well as being in charge of Wingham. He later become Editor of the AMJ.

Many of the students had suffered in various ways during the Second World War, which created a bond between them. David particularly appreciated their awareness of the wider world – something he had always found lacking in his Aussie peers. He found it a supportive, affirming environment.

It was the beginning of a new era, and for David it marked the point of his complete independence from Lora. His attitude of independent survival had intensified in the two or so years Lora was away from him as a teenager, and he was now ready to move out on his own.

Even though Lora had been anything but involved in David's life for a long time, she still found the new, independent, grown up David difficult to handle, and in a strange way, even though she had found him his position at Wingham, she was upset that he was so happy there. It was very obvious to Dr Winton that Lora did not understand how to manage her strong-minded "nephew", and, in fact, that she was going through separation pains or 'empty nest' syndrome without really understanding her own feelings.

Dr Winton was able to help her with some explanations and she gave in graciously and removed herself to Perth to retire, contenting herself simply to write weekly letters. For his part, David was grateful that Lora was able to let go, and their relationship improved with the distance.

But university was calling, and, as much as settling into Wingham was exciting, David had to begin his studies, and even more importantly, find some money to support himself. The first stop was an interview at the scholarship office.

"I need the living away from home allowance, please," said David.

"But you've only got one address here," said the official. "You must be living at home. If you're not, you'll have to give me your parents' address."

"I'm a war orphan," said David. "I don't have any parents."

And without further questions, the official warmly marked David's papers for the higher allowance.

Next, he had to talk to the scholarship officer about what course to enrol in.

"I'm thinking of doing science," he said, as he handed over his results from school.

"Oh, no," said the officer. "You did well in economics. There are hundreds of students in the science faculty, but economics is small, and new and exciting. Trained economists will be highly in demand in future years. You should do economics."

"Can I think it over?" David asked.

"You've got half an hour!" said the official.

Economics or science was not a simple decision of either/or. Economics was a four-year course, where science was only three. That would be another whole year without an income. Could David manage it?

Pondering, he walked out into the corridor, praying, and met a third year economics student that he had met the night before at the Evangelical Union's[4] 'fresher welcome' evening. They talked about the economics course for a while, and, before the half hour was up, David took this chance meeting as God's ruling in his life and went back in to sign up for economics.[5]

Both study and accommodation arrangements had fallen neatly into place. The government scholarship allowance in first year amounted to exactly the amount of David's fees at Wingham. Dr Winton was kind enough to offer David a reduction of 10 shillings a week if he would do things around the hostel, such as putting out

---

[4] The Sydney University Evangelical Union is a Christian group for university students that meets on campus with the aim of fellowship and evangelism to students and staff. Sydney EU began in 1936 and is still going strong today.

[5] David never regretted his decision to do economics and believed that it fitted him well for the range of ministries that God had in mind for his life.

the rubbish and looking after the hot water system. Compared to waiting and washing up at the Blue Mountains guest house, this was easy and David gladly agreed, earning himself extra money for expenses.

Wingham was the place for David. In Dr Winton he found an older, wiser, caring father figure who was secure in his faith. A quiet man, he smiled a lot, and it took a great deal to make him angry. He believed in the hostel, managed it well despite often limited funds, and frequently went beyond the call of his duty. Often, if students were left there on holidays, he would take them out around Sydney for the day. Sometimes he would need to help students who had got into trouble. One young man, arrested for stealing, was bailed out, and then sorted out gently by Dr Winton. In David, Ron Winton could see a young man in need of support and fatherly love, and he took him under his wing, encouraging him in things like the Bible study group he ran in the hostel and discussing any theological issues he had.

Dr Winton was not the only person David discussed issues with. Wingham boys enjoyed talking things over and David found an open, safe environment to discuss philosophical, faith and life issues in depth. He could think aloud about Christianity, ask real questions and ponder the consequences of his life of faith so far. As most of the other students were from completely different backgrounds and religions, he often was asked to explain the Christian position, and David began what would continue throughout his career - thinking through his faith and how to share it cross-culturally. As well as developing a more objective and adult view of Christianity, his close relationship with God was also growing as he continued daily Bible reading and began to write a personal prayer diary.

Finally, at Wingham, David found people he could really relate to, even though they came from Malaya, Indonesia, Singapore, India, Nepal, USA, Thailand, British North Borneo and Hong Kong.

'Harry' Huen Yeong Ching was David's room-mate in first year, and they got along famously. He wrote in David's autograph book: 'To my pal, David - Human races discriminate against each other on differences of colours of their skins and on their feeling of superiority over other races. If only all men spare some time to find out how immaterial our colours are in the eyes of God whose love is free for all, without any partiality. Our souls have no colour.'

David got along so well with Harry and the other students that his first year was taken up with more fun than study, and at the end of the exam period he was paying for it. He just passed most of his subjects, but failed one and had to sit a deferred paper. It was a rude shock, and he realised he would have to plan his study habits if he wanted to continue.

From second year on, David was seen less around the college, apart from meals or the occasional games of tennis and ping pong. One student's first memory of him at Wingham was going to see him in his room, where he was studying in a blue dressing gown.

But although he was not into college party life, his reputation was growing as a good counsellor. Other students respected him for his seriousness and would go to him for advice and a chat.

The maturing of his Christian faith and life found an outlet in the Evangelical Union on campus. David's gifts for leadership were developing, and, by the end of his first year of economics, he was elected Junior Vice President of EU. This position had particular responsibility for overseas students[6] in whom David had a natural interest.

In 1955, a group of Asian students wanted to start their own fellowship under the umbrella of Inter Varsity Fellowship[7], rather than just attending the general EU meetings. David could see that

---

[6] There were increasing numbers of overseas students in Sydney due to the Federal Government's 'Colombo Plan'.

[7] IVF or Intervarsity Fellowship was later known as the Australian Fellowship of Evangelical Students and was the wider umbrella body of Christian campus groups to which EU belonged.

overseas students, especially Asians, functioned differently from Australian students. They worked harder at their studies, and were much less involved in sport. They liked to get together to cook and eat Asian food, not very common in Australia in those days, and they had a lot of time to fill in on weekends.

Aussie outreach tended to be pretty direct, whereas the Asian approach needed to be gentler, building up more relationships. David was convinced that by having a Christian group especially for Asian students, not only would their needs for fellowship be met, but they would be able to reach out to other overseas students more effectively.

The group of students and David worked out together what would be a good arrangement, and then it was up to him to put the suggestion forward to the IVF General Committee meeting. It was a period when young people greatly respected their teachers and especially Christian leaders, and the EU was a conservative group. So it was a problem when some IVF committee members didn't agree.

"We shouldn't have specific ethnic groups – it will not promote fellowship," was the argument.

But David had become a clear thinker and had practised expressing his opinions calmly. He never had been short of words on something he believed was right, and a few years of debating at school had helped him hone his skills. The case was presented, it won the day, and, to his great joy, the Overseas Christian Fellowship came into being.

Later in that year he helped to organise a Christmas party in the home of the Women's Vice President of EU. Her family put on a terrific meal for the 150 students who came, many of whom began to come to the OCF.

In 1956, David became Vice-President of EU, leading the weekly teaching program. Up until this point, the program had consisted of unrelated talks from week to week, with 60 to 80 students attending.

David had also never been short of opinions on what he thought worked and didn't work, and he was not finding the EU talks helpful. He decided to make an appointment with TC Hammond, the principal of Moore Theological College, and the two met over sandwiches on Sydney University's front lawn one lunch time.

"I think it would be better to have talks that tie in to each other, and a program which is more planned out," David explained to him.

"What about a mix of expositional studies, with some other topics on different themes thrown in," suggested Hammond. "I'll give the first four studies myself!"

It was a start, but next on David's agenda was to work out a pattern of study groups in each faculty. Charles Troutman, the General Secretary of IVF, supported the idea, so David moved on to get the backing of the four EU faculty members. With encouragement from John McIntosh (arts faculty EU leader) and Royal Hawke (Veterinary Faculty leader) David had enough ammunition to present his arguments for what was, at the time, a radical new approach. One speaker would present a series of talks – expositional or thematic - and Faculty Bible studies would follow the teaching. The concept took off, and numbers grew radically. A few years later the EU had to move to a lecture theatre that would hold 800 or so students.

David's ability to organise was not restricted to EU. As the years at Wingham went on, David was given more responsibility, and often part of his job was gently and diplomatically recruiting other students to help out with things like tennis court maintenance or repairs.

He was also attending church at Christ Church, Gladesville, and found plenty of ways to bring his friends along. Victor Kijvanit, a student with a Volkswagen car with plenty of seats, was often on his list.

"Are you coming to church on Sunday, Victor?" David would say.

"Oh, I don't think so," was Victor's usual answer.

"But we need your car for transport for the other students," replied David.

"Oh, okay!" And Victor would end up driving his friends to church.

But life was not all study and Christian outreach. Something that was playing on David's mind very strongly was the question: was he going to be able to cope with life in the future?

The memory of the tears and sadness of the previous year had not gone away, even though Wingham had become a happy new home. He needed to know why he had cried for a full eleven months. Would he keep on crying? Would he ever really feel any better? Would he be able to cope with the challenges of life to come if he could hardly manage his Leaving Certificate?

First year economics was not a very time-consuming course in those days. David had plenty of time to spend in Sydney University's large library, particularly in the psychology section, reading about grief, loss and growing up.

He discovered some interesting things. The age of fifteen to sixteen is when the reality of loss sinks in deeply. Younger children can feel loss and grief, but in much less focussed ways. And while there were periods when David felt alone or sad in his early years, he had not truly grieved the loss of his parents, or the pain of his situation until he reached sixteen.

He began to understand that pains and losses from childhood needed to be resolved. His tears, even though he didn't deeply understand them while he was crying, seemed to be his outlet for properly grieving his losses, and letting all the hurt and pain out of his system.

Remarkably, discovering what had happened to him over that painful year brought him to thankfulness, rather than more grief.

Knowing that God had not only provided physically for him all those years, had saved his life numerous times, and now had provided the opportunity for him to grieve, was a freeing thought. In all the many difficulties and dangers, David had never turned to bitterness or to questioning God's plan. Now, in fact, he was more intrigued that God had let the grief happen.

"God is sovereign. And I am thankful," he thought to himself. "It's been dealt with and I can live a normal life."

And he was able to move on.

Chapter Ten

Young men are always invincible

Moving on from his pain was something David wanted to do, and he embraced his independence and the study and distractions of university life.

One distraction came on Sydney Uni Commemoration Day in his third year. It was a university holiday, when students typically found ways to upset the general public of the city. This year, two weeks before, there had been a huge confrontation between students and police, because the police had not been willing to put a zebra crossing across Parramatta Road next to the Uni. City trams and traffic crowded this main artery, and students daily took their lives in their hands crossing to the campus after alighting from their tram.

That week there had been three accidents, and rumours were flying that a girl, who had been knocked down by a car, had died in hospital. The enraged student body poured across the road at the rush hour time of 4.45pm and stayed put until 6pm, with traffic banked up for miles. Sydney CBD was brought to standstill, and the police were called in to move the students.

A zebra crossing was promised through a megaphone by the Commissioner, and the students dispersed, but not before a few arrests were made and Police Constable number 3619 punched a girl student, making her fall on the gutter and hurt herself. Law students threatened Constable 3619 with legal action, so all the arrested students were released.

But that was not the end. The students were going to make a statement. On Commemoration Day, the student body was divided into small groups, each with a responsibility for a different part of

Sydney city. Their task was to paint 'Beware of 3619' on pavements, billboards and all places visible.

David's small group was given the task of painting this protest on the north and south approach arches of the Sydney Harbour Bridge. This took some planning.

They arrived at the bridge at 1am, climbed over some barbed wire and clambered onto the arch above the road. At one point, the bridge painters' carriage overhung the arch, and, with thumping hearts, they crawled out onto the scaffolding, which was loose! As they were lying on their stomachs painting the sign, a black car – like a police car - pulled up, but it was only reporters who had been tipped off to take a photograph.

Finally, as the students climbed down the end of the bridge, two policemen standing next to their vehicle near the entrance to the bridge saw them and gave chase. David and his partners in crime tore through the nearby Fort Street Girls High School grounds on foot, doubled back to avoid the police vehicle, got into their own car and sped off down York Street. Because of the one-way road system, the police would have trouble catching them.

The Harbour Bridge sign was a success for the students. It took three days for the bridge painters to paint it out, and later the ineffective barbed wire was replaced with iron spokes. As for poor Constable 3619, he was so affected by the negative attention he had to take special leave.

Another distraction from study was the niggling pains that David was feeling quite frequently in the left hand side of his chest – almost between his ribs.

David went to see his friend, Dr Winton, to ask his advice.

"I'm getting pains in my chest," he explained. "I know I've got a heart murmur. Do you think it matters?"

Dr Winton decided that it was worth checking, so he set up an appointment with a Christian cardiologist, who was also friends with the Claydon family. Luckily for David the doctor waived his fee, and equally luckily for David, he had an ECG machine - about the best diagnostic tool on the market at the time.

He examined David and looked at the ECG results.

"Well, your blood is flowing in the wrong direction, which means you probably have a hole in your heart," he said. "How old are you?"

"19," answered David.

"Well, you'll live another 10 years, but not much past that," he said, matter of factly.

It was a shock for David. No-one wants to hear that he is going to die, much less a young man with his life in front of him.

On the other hand, he was still a teenager, and teenagers feel immortal. Teenagers also believe ten years is an eternity, and so the threat seemed a long way off. As David had already made his decisions about life, and was headed to a life of Christian service and ministry, the diagnosis didn't change his priorities or goals in any measurable way. In addition, David knew he had been saved from death so many times, and he thought "Well, I might even get run over by a bus tomorrow."[1]

In the end, it was more of a nuisance than a worry. And anyway, David didn't really have time to worry. The bulk of his free time was spent, as in the past, earning money to pay his bills. Holiday work added to his income, and he took one job doing administration tasks in an advertising agency, and another digging trenches for cables.

One of his more life-threatening jobs involved collecting fares as a conductor on the old 'toast-rack' trams. These trams would not meet today's strict work safety standards; David had to stand on a narrow platform outside the tram while it ran along, and a few times passengers pulled him in through the windows to stop him

---

[1] David really only thought seriously about the threat from his heart problem when he came to propose marriage to Robyn Hickin. He thought it was only fair to let her know of his diagnosis. When she said 'yes' he thought, "Well, we'll probably have five happy years or so together and that'll be it."

being hit by the mirror when a truck came close alongside.

The money was being earned, so David could live, but his life-long habits of economy allowed him also to save. By the end of third year at Uni, he had saved enough to take a trip overseas. His first year room-mate and good friend, Harry, had returned to Malaya[2] for health reasons, and invited David to stay with him in Ipoh.

It was a trip with a great deal less anxiety and stress than his last overseas journey from Palestine. Having Lora in Perth netted him a cheap train fare across the Nullarbor, because he was technically 'going home', and he then boarded a ship to Singapore with Harry's brother, Yeong Kong, who had become a Christian through Melbourne's Billy Graham Crusade. The two young men spent every evening of their peaceful voyage standing at the extreme front of the vessel, talking and enjoying the small breeze, and watching the white wisps of water which rippled and stirred as the ship cut through the water.

Harry's mother met them at the wharf and drove them up country, where things were a little more like David's old experiences. The ruling British were still trying to rid the country of Chinese communist terrorists, who had continued to fight for independence since the end of the war. Every time the car entered or left a British 'red area' the car was searched for medicines, food and terrorists!

But once this was over, the visiting began. Harry's family were welcoming and loving to David, sharing their culture and beliefs with him. Then it was off to Kuala Lumpur where David's current room-mate, Jim Rajaratnam, and his family entertained him. Malacca was next on the list, with the family of an OCF student, and finally David ended up back in Singapore, staying with another Wingham student.

[2] Malaya is now known as Malaysia.

Staying in Asian homes was an eye-opener for David, and gave him more insight into their cultures. He attended Buddhist feasts, visited Chinese temples, learned about Hinduism and Thai Buddhism, and experienced both Chinese and Indian customs, asking questions all the time.

After meeting with the leaders of the newly formed Singapore Varsity Christian Fellowship, and visiting various missionaries, including Alan and Shirley Cole, David returned home, with an article on Malaysian economics for the faculty Journal of Economics, and, more importantly, a new enthusiasm for making the gospel known in a culturally sensitive way.

But after the high of his holiday, David had to come down to earth again. There was still more study - one more year of economics – and then David had to decide what he was going to do.

Dr Paul White, the well-known Christian writer, was on the IVF Graduates Committee, and he and David became good friends. Dr White was famous for identifying certain Christian young men at university with talents and potential as 'Blokes Worth Watching'. David became one of his BWWs and White took it on himself to pray for him, encourage him and talk to him.

"What do you think I should choose for a profession? What job should I do?" was one of David's burning questions.

"All I know is that I've only got one gift," he replied, "and I ask God to help me use that gift for him. You've got to do the same."[3]

It was time to think hard. David knew that his life was going to be dedicated to Christian ministry in some capacity. He also knew that he needed to earn some money and put some savings behind him if he was going to do this. So true to his naturally organised personality, he decided to pursue a Diploma of Education, become an economics teacher and teach for five years.

---

[3] Most people would probably argue that Paul White had more than one gift, but David took his point; his purpose was to use his strengths and talents for God's service with God's help.

After that, he would be free to take on whatever ministry God saw fit to give him.

The Dip Ed was a boring year of study after four stretching years of economics, but David's church and EU activities, as well as extra responsibilities at Wingham, filled the gap. Dr Winton was showing himself to be a constant friend, and proved his care for him even after the study was finished.

Unlike today, when moving out of home is common for young people starting out in their professions, it was not the done thing in the late 1950s, nor could David have afforded to live by himself. Lora was still living in Perth, and David would not have wanted to go back with her anyway, so he had nowhere to live until Dr Winton invited him to stay in his own house next to Wingham.

David became young Mr Claydon, the only male member of staff at Kogarah Girls High School. The girls *seemed* very interested in economics, but they may have been more interested in their young auburn-headed teacher. Whether David appreciated the interest in his subject or in himself, teaching was something he was happy in.

As usual, he took an interest in the school Christian group, although he was not directly responsible for it. In the early days of his classes, two girls in one of his classes thought he was a communist, but later asked him about his beliefs. When they found out he was a Christian, they started to come to the ISCF group, and, during that year, the little group began to grow.

David had more plans for his career. He could see that, to become a Subject Master in the government school system, he would need to have some qualifications in accountancy, so he began studying an accountancy course at nights. [4]

He also had more plans for his general future. His university days had been full of study, work and Christian ministry, with no time or

---

[4] David sat for the accountancy exams and in due course was made an Associate of the Australian Society of Accountants – AASA

"David's" tram terminus where Sydney Opera House now stands

Robyn's last English lesson at Queenwood before the wedding, 1961

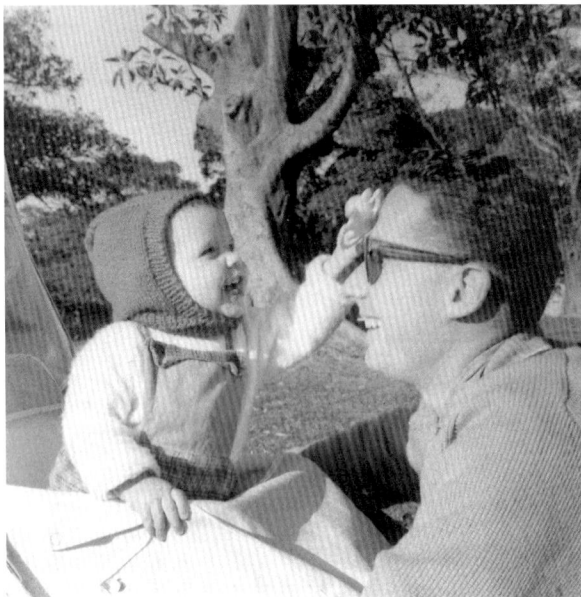

Kim 12 months old enjoying her daddy

David chairing Kairos

*Robyn & Marlene, Japanese night at Wyong
Crusader Camp, 1960*

Happy family, 1967

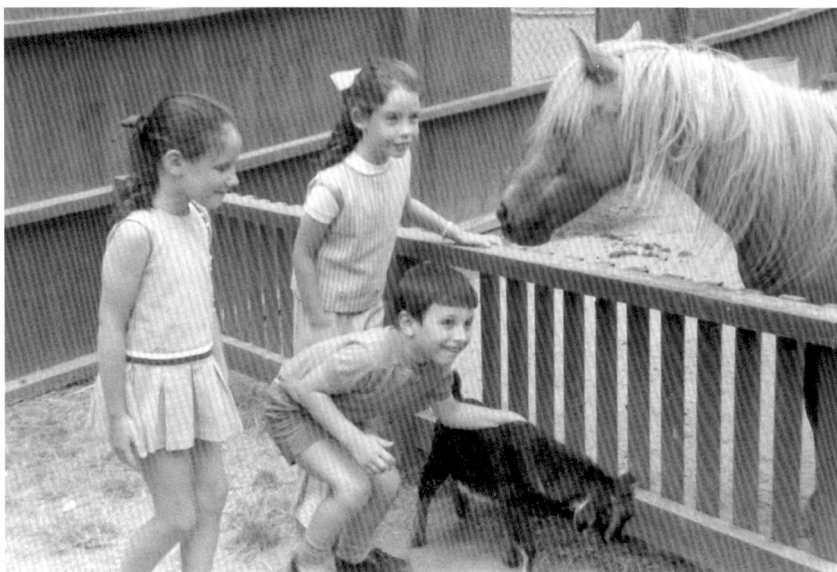

Kim playing with her cousins, Dana and Brad

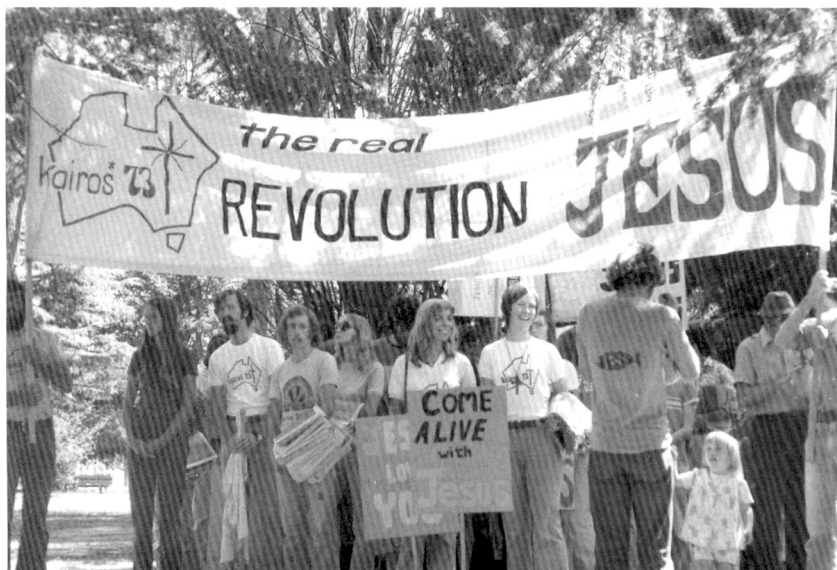

Kairos at Parliament House, 1972

The Kairos youth surrounding the (then) Parliament House in prayer, 1972

David talking with John Stott and Daniel Onwukwe of Nigeria at SU International Conference in Switzerland, 1967

Revd David Chan, SU ANZEA Regional Secretary

Robyn in her Abbotsleigh office

David & Kim at Abbotsleigh Centenary Garden Party

David speaking at training conference in Korea

David & Robyn at Abbotsleigh Centenary Ball

Mesulame Nainoca, first SU General Secretary in Fiji appointed by David, 1974

interest in girlfriends. He always knew he wanted to marry, and, at the age of about 23, with a secure full-time job, it was time to look around.

David had decided to join yet another Christian organisation. As well as being involved with the IVF Australian Committee, he joined the Church Missionary Society young people's organisation, the League of Youth. This was a vibrant group in the life of Sydney Anglicans, promoting the missionary cause and personal faith amongst teenagers and young adults.

Not surprisingly, David's leadership qualities were noticed, and he was elected to be its president in his first year. He then had to get to know the committee. Two names that kept coming up as great workers, good contributors and committed Christians belonged to two young women, daughters of a Sydney rector. In fact, the church their father was in charge of was the church that took the largest number of people to the Billy Graham crusades.

After some investigation, David found that the family was a loving and caring one, and the girls, Robyn and Marlene Hickin, sounded like vivacious and capable young Christian women, with a good interest in the wider world.

Now he just had to meet them.

CHAPTER ELEVEN

SETTING THE COURSE OF HER LIFE

Robyn Hickin, from being a happy, talented little girl with a clear Christian faith, had become a happy, talented and competent young woman with a deep, abiding trust in God.

Much of the development of her gifts and talents had to do with her parents. Madelon, who had been somewhat frustrated in her own opportunities as a young person, was quick to find plenty of opportunities for her daughters.

In 1948, when Robyn was thirteen, Madelon saw an advertisement in the paper for auditions for children to be part of a panel radio show. The programme, on 2CH, was called 'Juvenile Jury', and ended up being one of the most popular shows on radio at the time. Robyn auditioned and was chosen to be a permanent panel member.[1]

The panel consisted of five children, who were to answer questions sent in by other children about problems they were facing at home or at school. Using their vast wisdom and experience, the children on the panel would answer the questions on air, and then take questions from a live studio audience.

A sample question was: "I am always being teased about my freckles and this upsets me. What should I do?"

Answer: "I also have freckles so let's be proud of them because they make us different and special. After all we could say we have lots of beauty spots!"

Another question: "No-one plays with me at school. How can I get some friends?"

---

[1] Marlene, although much younger, was brought on as a guest juror occasionally. The program was sponsored by Persil, and Robyn can still remember the ads for 'Persil Whiteness', and actress Jeanette McDowell, who co-presented the show with radio announcer Brian White!

Answer: "Why not ask your parents to invite a couple of your school mates over to your home to play some games, or maybe go to an ice rink? This way they will get to know you and perhaps as a result include you in their group at school."

Her two years on Juvenile Jury gave Robyn a certain degree of fame at school and a great deal of confidence in speaking in front of audiences. The panel was often featured in the Radio Times, and once Robyn's birthday was celebrated in the Times in a photo spread of the children on the show.

Madelon could see Robyn gaining in ability and confidence, and soon she had a new task for her. Robyn came home from school one day, at the age of 16, to find that her mother had a throat infection. Unfortunately Madelon was booked to speak that night at a women's meeting. It was too late to cancel so she decided to recruit a replacement.

"Robyn, I can't go to the meeting, so you'll have to speak instead of me. I know you can do it," she said.

Robyn was quite shocked, but Madelon told her what she had planned to say and went over the talk with her several times. Then came the next shock.

"It's much better to look at people when you talk to them," she explained. "You shouldn't use any notes. You'll have to remember what you want to say – or use little palm cards if you really need a prompt."

The event made such an impression on Robyn that she can still remember the talk. It was about the way Jesus used His hands: hands that held children in love; hands that healed the sick with compassion; hands that turned over the tables in the temple with anger; hands that were crucified for our sake and hands that prepared breakfast for the disciples after His resurrection.

Whether Madelon intended it or not, her confidence in Robyn, her own example of using her gifts, and her mentoring of her for the task, was a turning point for Robyn, and was the beginning of a life time of public speaking – with no notes.[2]

But as well as mentoring her two daughters, Madelon also prayed for them. In future years, when both Robyn and Marlene were frequent convention speakers and preachers, they gave her a list of where they were speaking and what the topic was, knowing she would uphold them in prayer.

As Madelon got older, and, in later years when her eyesight was not as good, she said she didn't need lists any more but that she would still pray for them.

"Every morning when I wake I will say 'Robyn, Lord, Robyn' and 'Marlene, Lord, Marlene'" she said. "God will know where you are and what your needs are."

School was coming to an end and Robyn needed to decide what she was going to do. Her special interests were in English literature, acting and writing. Which would it be? Finally she decided that being a teacher would give her the opportunity to combine her interests and use all her gifts.

In her final year at Meriden, as the Senior Prefect and a House Captain, Robyn was now much less terrified of Miss Hannam. Knowing that a lot of boys from private schools went back after their final year and worked as junior teachers, she didn't see why she couldn't do the same, so she boldly approached Miss Hannam and asked for a job.

"I'd like to come back next year and join the staff of Meriden," she informed Miss Hannam. "Do you think it's possible?"

Miss Hannam was unruffled by the boldness of the offer but had a few suggestions of her own.

"I think you should go to Teachers' College or University first and then consider coming back," she said.

---

[2] Robyn still never uses notes and her ability to communicate imaginatively with people of all ages is commented on wherever she goes.

If Miss Hannam had realized what she would be missing out on at the time, she may have spoken differently, but Robyn took her advice and went to university. She went on to teach at other schools and never went back to Meriden.

Robyn started her Arts degree at Sydney University in 1955. As now, most people studied for their degrees full-time, and then found their first job. But Robyn's career was going to be anything but ordinary, again thanks to her mother.

When Madelon noticed an advertisement in the paper for a teacher in the Junior School at Abbotsleigh at Wahroonga, Robyn applied, and was offered the position, despite having no qualifications or experience. Switching day lectures to evening lectures at the university, her teaching career was off to a flying start. She took a fourth class in 1955 and started fifth class in 1956, but gave it all up in May, as Ronald Hickin had some exciting news for the family.

It was not unusual in Australia in the 1950s for the Australian-born to keep a great affection for England as the 'mother country'. Ronald had been calling England "home" for as long as Robyn could remember. As a family they had often talked about going to England one day, so when Ronald was offered a year's ministry in an English church, everyone was thrilled. Despite Robyn being 20, with a job and a full-time study load, the possibility of her not going with the family was not even considered.

St Giles in Ashtead was an evangelical parish[3] with a long history. For Australians, the sense of history in such places is extremely strong. The Hickins were provided with a house within walking distance of the church, which had a lych-gate, beautiful bells and a yew tree that was over 1,000 years old.

[3] St Giles may have been evangelical, but the Hickins soon discovered that evangelicalism in England had a different flavour from evangelicalism in Sydney, with more emphasis on church traditions.

Surprisingly, there were no romances for Robyn while in Ashtead, although the curate did attend her 21st birthday celebrations at the Royal Festival Hall to see 'Swan Lake'. Both Marlene and she made many friends amongst the youth fellowship, enjoying outings to Roman ruins and English picnics on heaths covered with bluebells.

The energetic family found plenty to do, even though their time in England was short. Robyn taught at Ashtead Preparatory school for a term and then decided to improve her musicianship. She had studied up to eighth grade piano in Australia, but felt she didn't really understand music theory. After several months, she sat the eighth grade theory exam through the Trinity College of Music, and passed.

Marlene found employment as well – she gained a teaching position for the year at 'Downsend', a prestigious boys' preparatory school in Epsom, and learned new skills, which set her up perfectly for a teaching position at Sydney Grammar Prep School on her return to Sydney.

The year was made even more exciting by a short trip to Europe. Ronald was representing the archbishop of Sydney at a conference in Budapest, Hungary, and so Madelon, Robyn and Marlene went to Paris for a few days to see the sights. Naturally, as a clergyman's family, they travelled on the cheap, staying at the YWCA in Paris. Like the price, accommodation was budget style, with dormitories consisting of beds divided by curtains. Breakfast was a warm bowl of milky coffee and a slice of bread. Following what others were doing, the girls dipped the bread into the coffee and ate it. The bread stuck to the roof of their mouths and the taste was most unpleasant!

Their excitement over, the family returned from England at the beginning of 1957, and Ronald took two temporary postings at St Matthew's, Manly, and then at St Barnabas', Broadway, before being appointed rector of St Andrew's, Sans Souci, in 1958.

As always, parish ministry became a family affair. Robyn energetically took charge of the Youth Group, with expert assistance from Marlene and from the young men from Moore College, who were curates or catechists at the time. One of these assistant ministers had some ideas, which Robyn had never heard before in either her family or at her 'girls can do anything' school.

"Because I'm a male," he explained to Robyn, "I should be leading the youth group and taking the Bible studies."

"I don't think so," she argued hotly. "What's so special about being male?"

"Well, what about a compromise," he suggested. "We'll be joint leaders. I'll take the boys for Bible study and you can take the girls."

"That's quite ridiculous," said Robyn. "I've got a reasonable amount of theology under my belt, and I fully intend to teach the Bible to boys as well as girls, just like I always have."

The young assistant reluctantly agreed, perhaps not thinking he should, or could, override the Rector's strong-minded daughter. Robyn's thoughts on this issue never changed, and in fact, gelled more firmly in years to come.

Robyn was a busy young woman. On top of her church activities, she had found a full-time position teaching primary school at Queenwood, a girls' school in Mosman. After a year she wanted to concentrate more on English teaching, and was moved to the Senior School in 1958 teaching English, Latin and Divinity. At night, she and Marlene were both studying for a teacher training course through the Teachers' Guild.[4]

---

[4] Robyn had well and truly caught the studying bug. After her Teaching Diploma she linked up with Armidale University as an external student to complete her degree, while at the same time also taking a few subjects a year towards the Th L until she graduated with Second Class Honours. After completing her Arts degree and the Th.L she enrolled in London University as an external student to do the Dip Ed. All these various courses were completed in 1971. Then in 1977 she began a Masters' Degree in English literature and language at Sydney University graduating in 1979.

Crusaders was the next thing on Robyn's list. Her desire to see a Christian group in her school had stayed with her since Meriden days, and she started a Crusader group at Queenwood, this time with the blessing of the headmistress, Miss Violet Medway. Soon 250 girls were regularly attending the Wednesday lunch time group.

With the 1959 Billy Graham Crusade being held in Sydney, Robyn took several bus loads of girls to the showground. Many of the girls made a decision to follow Christ. The weekly Crusaders group grew so large that over half of the senior students were attending, making a great impact on the school.

Just in case they didn't have enough to do, Robyn and Marlene used up more of their overflowing energy by running a Crusader camp at Wyong in the holidays. With the flow-on effect from the Billy Graham Crusade, they soon had too many students from Sydney schools for one camp and had to divide the camp into two. Marlene led one and Robyn the other, in different parts of Wyong.

Robyn was busy, committed and stretching herself. But at the age of 25 or so, with her career and her direction and priorities in life set, she was beginning to think about the future.

She had been praying, not *for* a husband, but that God would be with the man she would someday marry, guiding him and strengthening him in his faith. She trusted God to bring them together when the time was right.

And the time was about to become right.

Like many keen evangelical Christian young people of the time, Robyn and Marlene had a serious interest in foreign missionary work. They read missionary biographies, went to missionary conventions, and were very conscious of the importance of being available to God.

Towards the end of their time at Sans Souci, the two girls joined the CMS League of Youth. With a reputation for talents, hard work and commitment, soon afterwards they were both invited to join the League of Youth committee.

The new committee president was a dashing young auburn headed teacher named David Claydon. He also had a reputation for being a hard worker and a clear thinker. But even a good reputation is no substitute for knowing someone personally.

And Robyn didn't know him very well until the whole committee went up to 'The Grange' at Mt Victoria for a weekend retreat.

OF YELLOW JUMPERS AND ROMANCE

Acrisp, cold morning dawned over the League of Youth houseparty in Mount Victoria in December 1959.

Marlene and Robyn were sharing a room. It was warm in bed, and Robyn was enjoying the fact that she didn't have to get up as early as her sister. Poor Marlene was on breakfast orderly duty, but she wasn't feeling sorry for herself.

Escaping to her room away from her duties for a few minutes, Marlene desperately wanted to share her delight.

"Robbie, get up!" she said to her sister as loudly as she could without being overheard by the other campers.

"You'll have to get up and come out to the kitchen. David has this bright yellow sweater on and he looks gorgeous!"

The thought of this amazing sight was not quite enough to get Robyn out of her warm bed just yet. But God's plans were in motion, despite her sleepy state. Fortunately it was cold enough for the yellow sweater[1] to remain on for several hours, so she did have a chance a little later to see it for herself.

The David and Robyn story was destined to be played out on a larger stage than just breakfast in the mountains.

The houseparty went well; the committee got to know each other, and then Marlene had to go home early. David drove her to the station to catch her train home. She and her sister had not gone unnoticed by him over the weekend.

"These two girls are worth taking some interest in," he thought to himself. But he had to make a choice, and, for some reason, Robyn

---

[1] It was just as well David had friends with good taste who let him borrow their clothes. Due to his financial constraints he had never succeeded in getting together an extensive wardrobe, and the yellow sweater belonged to someone else!

seemed to be the one.

When the committee had dispersed, and David had returned to Wingham, he sent a Christmas card to Robyn. As a competent and dutiful committee president, he thanked her for her valuable participation on the committee! The next day he thought he had better send a Christmas card to all the committee, so Marlene received one as well.

But the first card had the effect that David was unconsciously hoping for. Robyn opened her Christmas card, was delighted, and rang David straight away.

"I know you don't have any family in Sydney," she said. "Would you like to join our family for Christmas lunch?"

It was not to be. David already had plans with the Uptons for Christmas. But he wasn't going to be slow off the mark, and Robyn had hardly any time to be disappointed before he added,

"I'm not doing anything on New Year's Eve. Could I come then?"

The arrangement was made then and there. It was exactly what Robyn had been hoping for. David, resplendent in a navy blazer[2] with gold buttons, joined the Hickins for their family dinner and midnight service on New Year's Eve, 1959.

If Madelon and Ronald had any misgivings about this young man with no obvious family ties who seemed interested in their daughter, they weren't saying. They were warm and welcoming, easy to talk to, Madelon had cooked a fabulous dinner and they seemed to like David straight away. For his part, he felt that he had found a wonderful family.

David was still serious, logical and a good planner. In his mind, he was telling himself, "These girls are the best members of the committee," but in his heart he was saying, "If this is God's hand, if this is the way forward, then I will keep praying and see what the Lord does."

---

[2] David's jacket was once again borrowed from a friend!

David headed off the next day to lead a Scripture Union boys' camp for two weeks. During that time Robyn came down with chicken pox, a most unattractive disease, especially for young people who are courting. Towards the end of her recovery, when she was no longer contagious, but still looked a sight, the door bell rang at the rectory. David and his friend, Lawrence Chia, had called in unexpectedly to see her on their way back from the boys' camp!

Robyn was in bed and came downstairs in her pyjamas and dressing gown, looking nothing like the girl David had last seen at her glamorous best on New Year's Eve. But he wasn't put off by a few spots or hastily brushed bed hair, and they had a good chat about her illness and his boys' camp.

David was now definitely sure that he was interested, and a few days later invited her to a social function at Wingham. Robyn went, met his friends and thoroughly enjoyed herself! The romance was on.

Ronald and Madelon moved down to Canberra soon after this, leaving Marlene and Robyn house-sitting in a garage flat in Castlecrag. David would turn up for a meal every weekend, and he and Robyn would sit and talk.

As they got to know each other, David began to appreciate not only Robyn's capabilities, but her positive attitude and cheerful energy. She was affirming and enthusiastic. She was friendly, open and a good listener.

Robyn was falling in love with David's quieter personality, yet still appreciating his sense of humour. She could see wisdom and abilities beyond his years. The two felt very well matched, and as they went on in life they became even more appreciative of the way God brought them together and used their gifts to complement each other.

They were getting to know each other's family too. David found the Hickins easy to relate to; warm, loving and full of interesting conversation, and he enjoyed the time they spent together.

For her part, Robyn was discovering Lora's affectionate side by correspondence. Lora seemed very happy to now have a 'daughter' to love, after a tempestuous, although improving, relationship with her nephew. David was grateful for Robyn's ability to love his aunt. In one letter to Robyn, Lora wrote,

"I have enclosed a photograph of myself which I would like you to have, as I am David's godmother. He has been so very precious to me all these years, and now I know and thank God for you, Robyn. David's whole being has been enriched and blessed by your life and Christian witness."

Apart from their families, David and Robyn's romance was not an obvious one to the people around them. David kept his own counsel at Wingham, rarely discussing his personal business. After a time, he gave up the League of Youth committee because of his new responsibilities with Scripture Union. As they went to different churches, and mixed in different social groups, not many people knew they were together.

But finally David knew the time had come. It was one of those perfect Sydney days in November 1960, with a bright sky dotted with cotton wool clouds. David had invited Robyn out to Middle Harbour, and the two were sitting side by side on a large rock, overlooking the water.

"I'd like to ask you a serious question," he said. "But before I do, I need to tell you two things which you'll have to take into consideration before you give me an answer. Firstly, I have a hole in my heart, and the doctor thinks I probably won't live beyond my late twenties. Secondly, I've been offered a job in Hong Kong, and there's every possibility I could take it and work overseas for a few years. But when you think about those, could you answer the question, 'Will you marry me?'"

Robyn might not have been expecting a proposal then and there, but her surprise didn't stop her saying "yes" then and there.

The problems with David's heart and health didn't matter to her. The possibility of living overseas was not an issue. Her affirmative answer was because she knew he was the right one, the man that God had brought into her life.

The wedding was planned for October 1961, almost a full year later. Robyn had school commitments with her final year classes that she was taking through to exams.

October 28, 1961, was the day for celebration for David and Robyn. St Andrew's Cathedral in Sydney was packed with their family, friends and relatives, as well as girls and boys from Crusader groups all over Sydney and a choir of girls from Queenwood school.

The wedding was over, and married life had begun. David didn't splurge on their honeymoon. He still had hardly any money! But a week in Surfers Paradise in the off-season was reasonably priced, and even budget accommodation is delightful for honeymooners.

David and Robyn were together. Young, enthusiastic and committed to God, they were hopeful for good things to come.

CHAPTER THIRTEEN

HOLDING ON FOR DEAR LIFE

When David met Robyn, he was an economics teacher earning more than £3,000 per year. When they married, he was a staffworker for Scripture Union, earning £1,000! David may have organised his 'five-year plan' of teaching in order to earn some money before starting in Christian ministry, but God had had different ideas.

Scripture Union was probably best known to the Australian population through the festival atmosphere of its beach missions[1], which were as much a part of the great Aussie camping tradition as striped awnings and kerosene lamps.[2]

Children of all ages and backgrounds, holidaying after Christmas with their families on sunny beaches up and down the Australian coasts, came along to colourful week-long programs on the beach and under marquees. There were Bible stories and games in front of sandcastle pulpits on the beach, lantern parades at night as well as singing, puppet shows, craft and competitions.

Teams of between 20 and 100 Christian young adults camped at popular sites to run the programs and share their faith gently with children who were getting bored with surfing and ice creams all day every day and wanted something else to do. Families would come back year after year to the same campsite because of the enthusiasm of their children for the missions.[3] Many Australian clergy in later

---

[1] Beach missions were officially known as 'Children's Special Service Mission' or CSSM. Irreverent young CSSM team members referred to it as 'Come Single, Soon Married' because of the numbers of romantic matches made on teams. The name was changed in later years to 'Scripture Union Family Mission' – which then became known as 'Single Until Finally Married'.

[2] This claim was made by the Sydney Morning Herald, 2 Jan 1971.

[3] It may also have been easy on the parents with ready-made 'childminding' built in. One local paper at a resort town, which was host to a beach mission team, mistakenly referred to CSSM as the 'Children's *Social* Service Mission' in 1971.

years said they first heard about Christ through Scripture Union beach missions.

The first beach mission ever had been held quite spontaneously on a Welsh beach in 1867 by Josiah Spiers, a creative young Christian. Amidst the hundreds of children enjoying their holidays, he saw a ready-made congregation that would respond to teaching that was appropriate for its age! He went to the children on the beach, rather than expecting the children to come to him at church. From his story- telling on the sand spread a worldwide movement of beach missions, camps, ISCF school groups and Bible reading 'helps' for children and families that would have a tremendous impact for Christ over the next century and more.

Scripture Union didn't take very long to reach Australia in 1879, with the first beach services held in 1888 at Manly in Sydney. After a few highs and lows in enthusiasm and organisation, it was a solid force in Australian evangelical life by the 1940s. Part of this was its very strong ties with IVF. Most Christian uni students took part in beach missions or led on camps. In turn, children converted at beach missions or camps would be encouraged to join ISCF groups at school, and from there become part of their university Christian group, completing the circle.

SU in the war years was headed by the very charismatic Vincent Craven. Craven had a special gift relating to young people and ran fantastic camps. Unfortunately his personal charisma was not accompanied by effective administration. By the 1950s, SU was in danger of becoming an old-fashioned nostalgic organisation. Adminstration was top-heavy and the organisation lacked focus.

To fix the problems, the talented Colin Becroft was called in from New Zealand. Becroft's main gift seemed to be selecting the right people for the job, and cutting back unhelpful structures. He trimmed the SU council from 29 to 12 and recruited younger, more focused staff with ability and potential.

One of these was David Claydon. Once he started teaching, David had not given up his university association with the Inter Varsity Fellowship, and was now its Prayer Secretary. Colin Becroft was Chair of the IVF Executive and he was impressed as he watched the 23-year old David in action. Everything he did seemed to be well-prepared, and, although a quiet person, he would happily meet new people in order to do his job better. David began to stand out in Colin's mind as a self-possessed and mature, independent young man.

In fact, he stood out as just the person to become the new Scripture Union Field Secretary. Becroft had discovered that his job as General Secretary of SU (NSW) and SU Federal Secretary was too much for one person, so he created a new position to release him of some of his load. The new person was to manage all the field work: children's ministry, schools, camps, Bible reading promotion, and country regional committees.

Colin cornered David at a meeting. "I have a great opportunity for you," he said. "I really think the job of SU Field Secretary is made for you; I want you to take it on."

But Colin didn't get the answer he wanted.

"I'm sorry. I just can't do that right now," David answered.

Colin tried again, but was again refused. David still had his five year plan in his head. He needed to get some money behind him to get married, and he had his eyes firmly fixed on Robyn.

Colin and David met each month at the IVF executive committee meeting. Even though he had had two refusals, Becroft was not going to give up. He pulled out the big guns.

"David, I'm sure that even though you've said no twice, you haven't prayed the matter through. I'm sure this is what God wants you to do," he said.

This third request came at an interesting time, coinciding with two other invitations. The first was from Hong Kong – to be an IVF staffworker. The second was from Mount Hermon School in Darjeeling – to be an economics teacher.

Clearly, God was saying something to David, and David decided he had better listen up..

David gave himself the weekend to pray and think it over, and then went over to his good friends, the Uptons, and talked it out and prayed with them. By the end of the weekend he believed that the Lord was directing him to accept Colin's invitation and join Scripture Union.

The post of Field Secretary was designed to relieve the hard pressed Colin Becroft of field supervision of Scripture Union activities – all the camps, school groups and beach missions around the State. This would have been a challenging job in itself; however, only a year later Becroft moved on to the United States and David found himself with bigger fish to fry.

Alan Kerr, the Federal Chairman of Scripture Union, had greatly appreciated Becroft's gifts and skills and couldn't see anyone else obvious to take over.

He asked: "Who are we going to get to replace you?"

"I've got a man," said Becroft.

"I find that hard to believe," replied Kerr.

Colin Becroft had anointed David as his replacement, and although they could see he was capable, the SU council felt they needed to find someone more mature and experienced for the job. While they searched, however, David was asked to take it on in an 'acting' capacity.

So at the age of 24, in 1961, David found himself acting in all three of Colin's posts as well as managing a staff of 35, of which he was the youngest member.

It was a huge job, and, by the end of the year, he confessed to Harold Knight (later Sir Harold) a member of the NSW Scripture Union Committee: "I feel like a man hanging on to a cliff face by the fingers, most of which have lost their grip."

But even if his fingers had lost their grip, God's hand was holding him up as he went about his new and challenging task. David had a long term commitment to full-time ministry. He also knew that the Lord had been working in his life and he had become convinced that God had led him to SU. If this was what the job had turned out to be, it was a matter of trusting God each day to give him the wisdom and grace that he needed. Robyn believed the same thing and her support helped him through the long hours.

Meanwhile, the council was still unsuccessfully looking for the more mature replacement. When at last they thought they had found the right person, he turned the job down. Finally, after a year, the council came back to David.

"We'd like you to apply for the position of General Secretary," they said. "Are you interested?"

David was interested in the job, but he wasn't interested in applying for it. "Well, I'm already on staff," he said. "And you can see how I work. It's really up to you to decide if you want me or not."

Whether he was their last resort or not, David soon began to make the General Secretary's job his own.

A normal day in the office began with prayers for all the staff. The rest of the day was filled with dictating letters, consulting with the field staff and answering phone calls. David had the gift of great output and efficiency, and he rarely wasted a minute. Even lunch times were spent with Committee members or donors.

The day usually finished around 6pm, but evenings were frequently occupied, either by phone calls or committee meetings. Both Keith Watson, the chair of the Children's work committee, and Bill Andersen, chair of the Schools and Camps committee, had lengthy agendas and spent many hours on the phone with David.

The committees were very important. Scripture Union was a grass-roots organisation, with many dedicated volunteers putting hours in on committees to run the variety of work. Getting on with the committee members was always going to be a crucial part of the job.

As in most groups, different people have different perceptions. Alan Kerr, the chairman, who had had so much respect for his predecessor, Colin Becroft, did not warm to David at the beginning. Whereas in Becroft he had seen mature self-assurance and ability with people, Kerr saw in David reserved self-possession and a formality which distanced him from others. Part of this may have been the age difference. David was younger by 20 years than most on the committee and still only a young man. Part of it may also have been the fact that he was actually very competent for his age and experience. He knew what he wanted to do, and he came in and did it.

On the other hand, Bill Andersen saw David consciously bring new warmth to staff relationships. Becroft himself had been criticised for what some saw as an attitude of cold purposefulness, where he would doggedly pursue points he was convinced about. David was aware of this and was quieter and more persuasive. Andersen saw him try to get people on side, judging reactions and mobilising support before starting something.

If anything hindered him, it may have been a lack of distinct charismatic quality compared to someone like Vincent Craven, who had carried the Scripture Union work largely by the strength of his personality.[4] Although David could give a good public address, he wasn't a 'star' in the same way that Craven was.

While he kept some of his cards to his chest, David was not jealous of other people's competence, and was largely understanding and trusting of his staff. Once he established that someone could do the job, he would not sit on his or her shoulder and watch, but

---

[4] According to Bill Andersen, 2005.

would affirm them or discuss problems later on.[5]

Although he may have appeared self-possessed, David was aware that his on-the-job learning curve was steep. He needed the ideas and wisdom of his very able team of Council members, and sought them out when he could. Once a week he was fortunate enough to lunch with Harold Knight[6], the Governor of the Reserve Bank and sought his advice on administration problems that were cropping up.

No matter what the first impressions, however, David became fairly quickly appreciated, despite the initial reservations of some of the committee. In fact, he fairly soon gained their admiration, not least that of Alan Kerr. He was clearly, and from the first, a person of a variety of gifts.

Firstly, he brought with him a good grasp of fundamental Scriptural principles and a prayerful desire to lean on God in all he did. He was good at the detail of organisation and administration, while also having the ability to see the wider picture and the vision to see possibilities, taking an informed, well-researched long-term view on every issue. But as well as being an ideas man, he was someone who got things done, especially by using his contacts from church, different denominations and IVF. Where he saw a challenge, rather than being stopped by it, he prayed and tried to think of a way around it.

Before Colin Becroft had left for the US, he had pointed out that marketing Christian literature in Australia was ineffective, because there was no adequate wholesale supplier. By 1962 David had talked it over with colleagues, negotiated some deals and presented good enough plans to Alan Kerr, the Federal Chairman, to be able to

[5] Denis McIntyre affirmed that David was a good delegator and an easy boss to work for.
[6] Harold invited David to replace him on the Board of a Christian printing company, Ambassador Press, and SU agreed so that his income would be increased through this. After some years David became Chairman of this Board and continued until some 30 years later when the company was sold to another printery due to the competitive nature of the industry.

establish Emu Book Agencies, a combined IVF-SU book agency.[7] At its peak Emu represented 18 major evangelical publishers, including Moody and Paternoster, the publisher of all the Dr Paul White titles. Profits from Emu were ploughed back into IVF and Scripture Union.

David also saw the physical needs of the organisation. By 1965 the old Elizabeth St headquarters was overcrowded and inadequate, but moving would have required much more money than was available. As David walked from the train station to the office each day he prayed.

"Lord, would you please provide one of these buildings that I'm walking past for Scripture Union – for your glory?"

When 129 York St came up, a series of negotiations, miracles and good financial plans allowed SU to acquire a building with plenty of room at the heart of evangelical Sydney.

Lack of finances was a continual struggle for Scripture Union. Camps, beach missions, Bible reading publications and general ministries took money to run properly, and there just never seemed to be enough. The pressure of limited funding and overwork can often put a depressing drain on energy and creativity, but David was never affected in this way.

SU had a strong prayer backing and David knew that, because of this, God would be faithful. In order to keep the praying people informed and to get more on board, he produced the first State news bulletin, a bouncy, optimistic typed sheet which spelled out the needs and the opportunities for SU, including practical ways for people to help. Somehow they got the donation levels up, and somehow they balanced the budget every year! His energy kept coming from whatever new development or challenge was just around the corner.

---

[7] Emu became known later as ANZEA Bookhouse.

There were some failures. Because the SU bookshop was not making a profit, David negotiated a change of leadership of the shop, but this was not successful. He was mature enough not to take the failures personally. In one way the committee structure was useful for this. He saw the work as very much run by the Committees and their very strong Chairs, and almost never felt personally responsible either for the failures or for the successes.

However, there were many successes. SU in New South Wales grew rapidly and steadily in the decade. In 1961, 5,000 school pupils were attending ISCF groups. By 1970, there were 9,500 in double the number of groups. In 1961, 2,800 children had been contacted by beach mission teams. In 1971, 11,000 were contacted by beach mission teams, and the number of teams had increased from 30 to 50. Camp numbers had increased, Bible reading notes were increasing, and churches of all denominations were behind them as they saw the usefulness and the opportunities of SU ministries to their own members.

The challenge was not only to keep the current ministries functioning well, but also to look into the future. David wanted SU to get up front, stay up front and speak relevantly to the modern times.

CHAPTER FOURTEEN

SETTLING DOWN TOGETHER

Working intense hours and under pressure, as well as being in the first year of marriage with little money, is not normally a recipe for health or long-term happiness, but Robyn and David seemed to settle down very harmoniously together.

Their family was supportive. Lora had helped them out immediately when their negotiations to buy a house were delayed. Lora may have been a woman with no money, but she had both contacts and inbuilt authority. She rang a retired minister friend and stated confidently, "Robyn and David need somewhere to stay for about a month until their house comes through." Immediately short-term accommodation was found until the young couple could settle at Ryde where they lived for 6 years.

Madelon and Ronald Hickin were also helpful. When a block of land came up for sale in St Ives, Madelon saw it and told Robyn. In due course they bought, built and enjoyed their new home for many years.

David's job at Scripture Union was not the only new one. As was common for those days, Robyn left her job at Queenwood when she married in 1961. For the next two years she took on one of her great loves in life and became the Girls' Organizing Secretary for the Crusader Union.

This was going to be replaced by an even greater love very soon. Two years after their marriage, in 1963 David and Robyn were blessed by the birth of their only child.

Fathers were not encouraged to be in delivery rooms, so while Robyn laboured David paced up and down outside.

"Mr Claydon? It's a girl," came the call, and David rushed in to look with wonder at his beautiful little daughter. As Robyn held baby Kim, she summoned up enough energy to say to Dr Neville Babbage, "She will be a brave Crusader".[1]

Kim was an adored baby for two young parents who also adored each other. When she was a few months old, Robyn wrote to David while he was on a trip away: "I have thanked the Lord over and over again for you and for her. I couldn't feel happier or more wonderfully blessed than I do at the moment, and I am so thankful that the Lord chose you to be Kim's father, because I know that there is no one else in the world who could be good enough for her."

David went away frequently with his SU job, both around the state visiting SU work, and to camps and beach missions. The separations were not easy for either of them. One Christmas Day, having just left for Beach mission, he wrote to Robyn; "I felt very sad leaving you and Kimbo behind, but I didn't like to tell you because it would have made you sadder, so I just bit my lip and am still biting it."

But despite these pangs, the young Claydon marriage was continuing well. Almost unbelievably, and unlike the majority of married couples, David and Robyn developed a pattern of discussing issues together and never arguing, which has continued to this day.

Even Kim, the person who ought to know best, agrees that David and Robyn have never argued.

"What do your parents do when they disagree?" she was once asked.

"They go rather quiet," was the most scandalous answer she could give.

David and Robyn seemed to be blessed by having easy-going temperaments, despite their driven-ness in their work, and although they had serious discussions and talked things through, they both contend that they have never really disagreed on anything.[2]

---

[1] This was a line from a Crusader hymn Robyn and David had frequently sung. Robyn's words were proved true; as a teenager Kim would be the Crusader leader at Abbotsleigh School.

[2] David's comment about this in later years was, "I can't imagine what you'd fight about."

Perhaps the reason for their harmonious relationship was the very high respect they both had for each other from the very beginning. David always had the highest regard for Robyn's talents, and this regard only increased as he encouraged her to take opportunities and use her gifts. For her part, Robyn was impressed by David's quiet efficiency, clear thinking and plain speaking. When you add in their intense love for Christ and commitment to him, they clearly had a strong 'rope of three cords that will not break'. [3]

The only real sadness in these early years of their marriage was waiting for more babies that never came.

Robyn had loved growing up with her adored sister Marlene. The two were close and the best of friends all their lives. She dearly wanted Kim to have the same bond with a sibling, but it was not to be. Six or seven years of waiting and hoping had produced no more children. Finally a gynaecologist confirmed that Robyn was unable to conceive again, and Kim would be an only child.

With God's grace, Robyn and David were able to accept the loss of their hopes, and, as time went on, they even became grateful for it. Kim had a surrogate brother and sister in her two cousins who lived close by for some years before their family went overseas. Kim's relationship with her parents was unique. The three Claydons became a little unit of equals together, rather than feeling a separation between parents and child.

Extended family was an important part of their lives. At Christmas, on birthdays, for celebrations of all kinds and on most weekends they would visit Robyn's parents, her aunt Lilian Arrowsmith (she of the Friday chocolates) and David's Aunty Lora.

Lora had decided to move back to Sydney once David was married, living in the inner west of Sydney and working as a deaconess at Parramatta. David made a point of visiting her weekly from about 1967, but because of his hectic work schedule, he couldn't set a consistent day or time. Ironically Lora, who had spent her life turning up unannounced, found this a little hard to take.

David's work schedule had plenty of potential to create disharmony in the family. As well as the trips away and the long hours in the office, he had Committee meetings in the evenings – at least one every week and usually two, usually lasting until very late.

David remembers Robyn being gracious in coping with it, and Robyn doesn't remember ever feeling resentful. That was David's work, and that was what God had called him to. However, it didn't stop her penning this ditty about him in 1964.

Most wives could ring their husbands,
At any time I'm sure,
They'd merely dial the number
They'd have to do no more.
But it seems that I am fated
Every time I try to ring
And say, "It's Mrs Claydon –
Is my husband in?"
To be told, "He's in a conference"
Or, "Talking on the phone".
And "Could you ring back later?"
Is said in dulcet tone.
Sometimes I'm feeling braver
And with great temerity, ask
"What about Miss Whitfield,
Could she just speak to me?"
And so I leave a message
And regretfully hang up.
Perhaps next time I ring him
I might have better luck!

Despite his busy schedule, David did still want to see his two special ladies. Mornings seemed the only available time, so after a while he changed his office hours, usually going in about morning tea time. Once a week or so he arrived in time for prayers at 9 am.

To make things a little more hectic, both David and Robyn were studying. Although he had good Christian teaching growing up, David had always felt the need to have a sound theological base. Now that he was in fulltime Christian work this seemed even more of a necessity, even though he wasn't considering becoming ordained. David had no money, time or inclination to pursue fulltime theological study, so he decided to enrol in a Bachelor of Divinity, through the Melbourne College of Divinity, and do a few subjects each year, studying at night.

Having a husband almost completely occupied by study and work might have been a problem for Robyn. There wasn't much on the newly invented television she liked to watch to keep herself amused. So, about this time, she decided to study for her Th.L. Their relaxing time in the evenings was spent reading or discussing theology, or playing scrabble in Greek to help push their Greek along.[4]

With much of their marriage based on respect for each other's abilities, David and Robyn quickly fell into the habit of encouraging each other to take opportunities.

Even though Robyn had started a teaching degree, she had never completed it, doing shorter, smaller courses for her teaching qualifications. She decided to pursue a degree, which she could do by correspondence through the University of New England, except for one problem: she would have to attend two-week intensive on-campus study periods twice a year for a few years. With a little girl at home, this was looking impossible. David could see how

---

[4] David studied his Hebrew courses by putting the vocabulary and verbs on a tape recorder and playing the tapes as he drove around the State for SU work.

important it was to her. "If your mother can help out during the day, we can get through this," he told her. "I think you ought to do the degree."

The next problem was the weekend in the middle of the two-week intensives. Robyn wanted to come home, but Armidale is a good seven-hour drive from Sydney. Even though they didn't have much money, David decided there was a way around it. "I think you should go by plane, and then fly home for the weekend," he told her. She did, and she completed her degree.

The next opportunity for David was a Fellowship from the Winston Churchill Memorial Trust. This was a new scholarship award, set up to further research in professional fields, providing money for successful applicants to study overseas.

Like her mother before her, Robyn always had an eye open for possibilities. As she read about this new award in the paper one morning, she thought, "David ought to apply for this".

David agreed. Schools in New South Wales were about to introduce a sixth year of high school, making school leavers another year older and changing school dynamics. David felt that Scripture Union's ISCF Christian groups were generally unprepared to relate to older pupils, so he applied to do a study of British, Singaporean and American senior students and how they formed their values.

The Fellowship allowed for not only theoretical research but hands-on experience. David decided he could also get some experience of the British Scripture Union's Sixth Form subject-related camps, as well as have a look at the American camping program, which seemed to be exciting, attracting older teenagers.

Scripture Union didn't mind David applying for the Fellowship. As well as getting some useful experience and research done for themselves, the timing fitted in with the SU International Conference in Switzerland, which they thought he should go to, but couldn't pay for. David took his $2664 award, went to Singapore,

Malaysia, the UK, Switzerland, Canada and the US, did his research and wrote his paper.

The big down-side was the four months away from home, and although Robyn had encouraged David to go, she still found it very hard, especially as Marlene and her family were overseas. At one stage, Kim, who was only four, contracted measles. Robyn, sitting up all night with a sick, feverish child, was very mindful of the fact that she was alone and prayed for God's strength for herself and healing for Kim.

Thankfully Kim recovered, Robyn managed, and at the end of the study tour David came home to the title of 'Anglican of the Week'[5] and to the biggest hugs a four-year old and a loving wife can give.

For all it achieved, however, the Churchill Fellowship did bring a different sort of problem to the fore. As David met with people in the various overseas settings he was often asked about himself. For a long time, he had been careful not to reveal any details about his past. People like Dr Winton, his mentor for seven years, and whose house he had shared for two years, was aware of only some of the details of his growing up years. Colin Becroft thought that David had spent his pre-university days in WA. Bill Andersen of Scripture Union thought at the time that David was quite confiding, but years later realised he knew a lot less than he had thought.

Keeping his past private was the way David was protecting himself. The simple fact was that he was unable to tell any part of his childhood without tears completely overwhelming him. Because of this, David rarely talked about himself; he dreaded and discouraged questions. He was much happier discussing other people, or work, or ministry.

But because his story was so unusual, and so fascinating, anyone who heard even part of it wanted to know more. "Don't you have any idea who your parents were? Have you ever looked for them?

[5] From *The Anglican* newspaper, November 24 1966

How did you get out of the orphanage? You honestly don't know how old you are?" were some of the questions he was asked.

Because of his reluctance to answer and his almost firm refusal to give any information, rumours began to swirl about his origins.

"He was rescued from a rubbish dump in Jerusalem" was one story.

Even more incredible was the question: "How much did Deaconess Claydon have to pay to free you from the Arabian child slave camp you were in?"

The questions were unending and David often felt exploited.

"They want to know about my life because it's interesting, not because they care about me," he thought to himself, and he started to see anyone who wanted to know as an intrusive interrogator.

Family was different. Telling Robyn and the Hickins had been difficult to begin with, but had become much easier. Marlene particularly was very keen to know about David's experiences, and David shared a lot with her and Robyn in their courting days. In the context of supportive love and caring, he became sometimes even happy to reflect on what had happened to him. But this happiness didn't extend to the outside world.

In 1967, in preparing for the Churchill Fellowship, David began to get anxious. His main concern about the trip was that, as he visited groups and schools, people would ask him about his background and he would cry in public.

The only thing that had ever worried Robyn about marrying David was that one day he might find his background all too much to handle, and would not be able to cope.

She became his main encouragement to get past this hurdle.

"You've told me your story," she said to him. "Even though you cry about it, you've come to a point where you can see that God has been at work in your life, regardless of circumstances. Why not let others see that too?"

David began to see his story from another perspective. Robyn gave him the confidence to answer people's questions, while he distanced himself emotionally from it to stop the tears.

Of course, the questions did come up on the trip. People asked, and he started to respond with some details. It was the first time he had ever told anything about his past without tears overwhelming him. But it was not a complete breakthrough. It would be another ten years before he could talk without moisture welling up in his eyes. And he would be well into his fifties before he could talk at all freely and without tears, although he still felt the pain inside.

Finally, David was able to see that sharing his story as a ministry tool could actually help and encourage others. This was especially true for young people. Many years later, David and Robyn were speaking at a church in Croatia when David noticed a large group of teenagers milling around at the back.

"Who are they?" he whispered to the pastor.

"They are all war orphans. They have lost their parents in the fighting," came back the sad reply.

"Can I speak to them afterwards?" asked David.

So at the end of the service, David brought them all forward. Through a translator, he told them that he too was a war orphan.

"God has been so gracious in my life," he shared. "While I know how painful it is to lose your parents, I also know that God will always love you and be with you in every situation. You don't ever have to feel alone."

There were many tears and hugs in the church that night.

But his story encouraged more young people than just orphans. On a trip to Nepal in 1993, he was visiting the school students of the Kathmandu Study Centre. Most of these were children of missionaries working with the United Mission to Nepal, and many of them felt hard done by having to live in one of the poorest countries in the world, and continually move between cultures and lose friendships.

"I know how tough it can get," he said. "But no matter how tough you think your situation is, God does care. In fact, with God, you can override almost any loss and be an achiever."

Just about every child must have gone home and told parents about this strange orphan made good, because, over the next few days, David had parents coming to him in tears, thankful for the positive impact he had made on their children.

Although it would take many years, his losses and griefs as a child were becoming a gift of encouragement to others.

CHAPTER FIFTEEN

FLOWER CHILDREN AND FEDERAL SECRETARIES

Canberra was awash with flowers and flower children on the first weekend of March, 1973. Members of Parliament turning up for work on the Friday were all given pink carnations by long-haired, beaded, t-shirt-wearing young people with a message to spread. If the MPs had looked out of their office windows to see the 10-foot high cross erected in front of Parliament House, they would have been in no doubt whatsoever what that message was all about.

The Jesus People were in town.

The late 1960s and early 1970s was the protest and drop out era in the western world. Young people didn't want to follow the status quo or fit into the mould. They wanted to be creative, to be different, to do what seemed 'right for them'. And they seemed to be dropping out of traditional church structures by the dozens.

The 'Jesus Movement' began in the US by Christians who were looking for a way of reaching this growing number of young people who were more and more against the traditional patterns and structures of church. It was characterised by informal fellowship, little hierarchy and acceptance of the music and dress of the day.

As do most things from the US, the Jesus movement spread to Australia. A variety of ministries to youth were started in shop fronts or other non-church locations and the mood spread across the country. The groups were scattered and haphazard until David Claydon played a part in bringing them together. A national conference on youth ministry[1] led to a demonstration day, named 'Kairos', Greek for 'special significance'.

[1] Surprisingly, the conference was paid for by the government. David Claydon was nicknamed 'honeytongue' after this because it was his sweet negotiating which had found the funding.

Two and a half thousand young people arrived in Canberra from all over Australia for Kairos 1973, timing neatly with the opening of Parliament for Whitlam's new government. Carrying banners and placards reading slogans like, 'The real revolution – Jesus', 'Come alive with Jesus', and 'Jesus is the way', they marched to Parliament House where Mal Garvin spoke: "We are not here to protest anything, but to demonstrate Jesus is alive, and there is a way!" The young people sat and listened to singers and speakers, and then surrounded Parliament House holding hands and praying for the new parliament and for Australia.

Somewhat surprisingly, conservative-looking David became the chairman of this Kairos '73 gathering. He was still young, but unbearded and not noticeably trendy[2], and yet he was dubbed the 'Pope of Australian Jesus People' and 'the only short-haired Australian Jesus Freak'.[3] Part of his contribution to Kairos, as well as organising, was to move amongst the young people on the day, encouraging them to pick up their rubbish as they went through Canberra, to leave behind an impressive message to the city that Christians are not just all talk.

David had developed his contacts with the Jesus people through his new appointment in 1971 as Federal Secretary of Scripture Union. It was a different job from what he had had before. General Secretaries of each State kept the various local ministries running well and handled finances. The Federal Secretary position was more of a general leadership and visioning role, co-ordinating national policies and producing materials.

Up until now, this job had only ever been done on a part-time basis, but SU had grown so much in the 1960s, all over Australia, that it needed someone to bring the movement together at a national level.

---

[2] Sydney Morning Herald, reporting on the new image of SU, 28 Sept 1973
[3] From a New Zealand SU brochure, and Mike Eastman of Frontier Youth Trust in Britain.

The SU Federal Council who invited him had faith in the leadership he had shown so far. He had shown SU in NSW 'genuine spiritual leadership' and had given them an 'unending supply of drive and enthusiasm'[4], as well as doing all his tasks with meticulous thoroughness.[5]

But there was a large task ahead. And to achieve it, David turned first to prayer. Praying through decisions and setting and praying through a few priority goals for each year had become his established pattern and the way he worked out God's will for his life and annual program.

His days were varied. In one week, David spent time with the SU staff in Adelaide, thinking and praying through their schools and youth work and attending a beach mission training afternoon. Getting back to the office, he pored over piles of correspondence, including letters about: Western Australia needing another schools' worker; Tasmania wanting a statement about the importance of ISCF in schools to give to principals; Victoria describing youth work training development and asking for comments; a job enquiry; and an interstate request for one banner style for all the SU-CSSM beach mission teams around Australia.

Phone calls and meetings about such things as printing ISCF brochures, drafting of Bible reading materials, making SU badges, and of course finance and committee meetings, conspired to take up the rest of his time. He frequently worked at home to get his thinking and writing done free of distractions.

David's 'imaginative administration'[6] was earning him credibility amongst different Christian groups. However, he was in a job which was very difficult. Almost no-one who had done it before him had been terribly successful.[7] The Federal Secretary had to be seen to be

---

[4] SU News April 1971 p2
[5] John Prince *Tuned into Change* preface
[6] Gerald Davis characterised his leadership in this way in *Church Scene*, 15 Aug 1974
[7] According to Alan Kerr, 2005.

visionary and a strong leader, yet also allow the local SU bodies to take the reins when it came to doing things.

David's role was about articulating a vision, convincing others – SU staff, committees and supporters - to get behind it, and helping the different States find ways to achieve these things.

But David had always been both a person who could see ahead, and a person who got things done. For him to find himself solely in an advisory role was to find himself removed from what he was best at – achieving his outcomes.

Alan Kerr perceived some rumblings amongst State Secretaries about what could have been seen as an authoritarian attitude from David, as he came in as the 'expert', knowing how to do things.[8] However, if there were any rumblings, they weren't communicated very far. Dr Bill Andersen, Federal Council chair for seven years, was never aware of it. He asserted later that there were no serious criticisms of David and no serious policy failures in his time, and that he "was much appreciated."

David did a lot to help SU think more in terms of being an Australian body, rather than separate State bodies. When he began as Federal Secretary, it was the first time that every State had had a full-time General Secretary. In 1976, he was delighted at the annual Federal Council having "a real sense of its being a national team".

He wrote after the council meeting, "We were strongly reminded that, if we stop day by day and take time to study God's word, we will get a glimpse of his glory, his sovereignty, his grace and his love. As this vision or knowledge of God continues to deepen, we seem to be continually refreshed in our determination to be his disciples in this world."

David was both determined to be that disciple himself, and to help others be it as well, as far as he could. This meant keeping

---

[8] For all Alan Kerr's early opinions about David's abilities in a figurehead role, he still thought very highly of him, and even wrangled unsuccessfully at an international committee to have David become SU International Secretary.

Scripture Union fresh and relevant, thinking through the organisation itself, researching strengths and weaknesses, and addressing some of the changing social trends.

Youth work was one of the things that had to change.

Scripture Union had to shed its image of earnest young men in tweed jackets and distinctive lapel badges distributing tracts to children. In its place came the 'Theos' missions to young people, run by a whole range of different looking people, including trendy long-haired youth workers who slept under their surf-boards.[9]

"We don't live in a monochrome society," David said in one interview. "There are many cultures and we need youth workers who can minister in each one of them."[10]

By keeping connected to the development of the Jesus Movement, he stayed close to where the mood of the day was heading, and was able to plan more relevantly for things like the leadership training conferences for ISCF Leaders.[11]

Another changing social trait was a lessening loyalty to organisations. Where Christian school students previously were keen to belong to ISCF, by 1974, their mood was anti-organisation and anti-establishment. By 1976 students seemed apathetic, and Christian teachers were over-burdened. The SU school work was starting to look irrelevant. But rather than trying to generate support for the group, SU decided to challenge Christian teachers and students to be 'faithful to God' at school, and not so concerned with ISCF as such.[12] To reinforce this, David called for Christians around Australia to pray and support Christian teachers in State schools.

[9] Sydney Morning Herald 28 September 1973
[10] Church Record 15 November 1973
[11] He also began the 'Easter Academy', run for a few years with Robyn's help, inviting ISCF leaders in their final school year and the previous year school leavers for an Easter weekend training event, aimed at preparing them to take a leadership role in the life of their churches. Robert Forsyth, now a bishop in Sydney's Anglican Diocese, was one attendee of the Easter Academy.
[12] *Outreach* SU Magazine July/Sept 1974

SU also introduced a new program for schools called 'The Christian Option' in Tasmania, which became accepted as a normal part of the social science high school syllabus. Every student, whether Christian or not, was able to hear the gospel in social science classes as part of school work.

A staple element of Scripture Union had always been its Bible reading notes and the priority it placed on the Scriptures. David himself had grown up reading the Bible every day, helped along by SU notes. In the 1970s, however, fewer and fewer people were using them.

"We are convinced that God's people need to study His word systematically and with understanding," David wrote.[13] It was especially important to get some useful and child-friendly Bible reading materials out into the public. After prayer and a few setbacks, David encouraged John Lane[14] to produce a new children's series entitled *Start Look and Listen*, which became very well received.

Some issues had to be re-thought altogether. One of these was how God relates to children. A recent book by Goldman on how children understand Christian truth argued that children could not absorb the conceptual content of their faith. And at church gatherings, whenever an SU worker would speak about taking the gospel to children, this question always came up:

"What about the children in third world countries with parents of other religions? If they die in childhood without hearing about Jesus – will they go to hell?"

Scripture Union needed to have a biblical base for responding to these questions, so David wrote and thought, and asked others to write and think on the issue for the benefit of the whole organisation.

Many of these social trends were related to an apathy which had settled on Australian culture from the mid-1970s. The protest era of

[13] *SU News* 1976.
[14] John Lane was General Secretary for SU Victoria and an expert in children's ministry

the early 70s had not lasted for long. Now sluggish economic conditions, an explosion of societal issues such as poverty, and what David called a new form of individualism – 'uncommitted collectivism' where people wanted more rights but fewer obligations - were causing people across society to look inward.

This was also a feature of the Christian culture, which was putting more and more emphasis on the importance of the family. As society's issues increased, so too did the number of groups set up to answer the issues. This meant less energy and loyalty for SU, and more fatigue as Christians tried to look outwards.

David was trying to get SU to respond to the issues. In 1978 he gave a talk replying to the big-news event, the Henderson report on poverty. In 1979, capitalising on the International Year of the Child, he gave a week of ABC radio addresses entitled 'Children have much to give'.

But even more importantly, he wanted to establish a place which would give more than one-off replies to the issue of the day. He wanted Christian thought to contribute positively to the national dialogue about community values and issues.

So in 1977 David, with the encouragement of Alan Kerr, set up the ZADOK National Study Centre in Canberra. It became a joint project of Scripture Union and the Australian Fellowship of Evangelical Students.[15] Its aim was to attract people to come and study contemporary issues in Australian culture and society in the light of Scripture.

With tapes and papers, short courses and seminars, the centre was set up to help Christians to be more Christian in the way they worked, lived, played and participated in community and national affairs. There were one or two-week courses for specific groups of people, for example, young graduates, lunch hour or evening lectures for Canberra's public servants, weekend seminars for people

---

[15] AFES was the new title for the old IVF organisation.

from inter-state and evening seminars in different State capitals.[16]

Despite the new challenges in Australian culture, Scripture Union was still moving ahead, and, in 1980, it celebrated a milestone: its hundredth birthday.

SU Australia had become the largest facilitator of Christian lay people to be involved in evangelistic and nurture ministries. From 1971 to 1979, SU staff increased from 59 to 104 across Australia. In 1975, 7129 volunteers on beach missions, camps and in ISCF groups did the equivalent of the full-time work of 532 people for a year. By 1979, that number of volunteers had grown to 10,000.[17]

Rather than being threatened by it, as had happened a generation previously, churches across denominations were more and more appreciative of the ministries of this Australian national movement.

And it was touching people's lives. On the occasions when David and other SU workers would come across people who had met Christ or been affected through their ministries, they were delighted. Some years after David had first started his work with SU, he met new team members who had come to know Christ when they were children at a beach mission, many years before.

The impact Scripture Union had on individual lives was untold. The many thousands who were converted at beach missions, the children who grew and were nurtured in their faith at camps, the people who had gained a deepened spiritual walk through the Bible reading material - all these were, and still are largely unknown, except to God himself.

The centenary provided a wonderful opportunity to look back and see what God had done through the organisation in people's lives, but as always, David emphasised the need to look forward and

---

[16] Zadok was the name of a priest who had a key political role in the time of King David. As a model of political skill and persistent faithfulness to God, Zadok was thought an appropriate namesake for the study centre. ZADOK still exists as an organisation of about 750 people and is now based out of Melbourne. See www.zadok.org.au

[17] SU News February 1979

to do the task with "the energy and enthusiasm that comes from the working of the Holy Spirit in us".[18]

He would need that energy and enthusiasm of the Spirit. There would be more for him to do... and much further afield.

---

[18] Speaking at the Centenary Rally 20 July 1980 in Sydney, as reported by Ramon Williams in New Life 28 August 1980. Williams finished his article writing, "If the supporters of Scripture Union are as enthusiastic as the staff and voluntary workers, SU can face the future and the new programs full of confidence. Its influence on the growth of Christian lives and the evangelism of this country should see much progress over the next 100 years."

CHAPTER SIXTEEN

SCHOOL, TRAVEL AND PAGEANTS

When little Kim was old enough to go off to school in 1968, Robyn went with her – as a teacher.

It was back to Queenwood, where Robyn had taught before her marriage. This time she had taken a step up to be head of English, and, in the last two years, Deputy Principal.[1] Robyn and Kim travelled happily every day by car from St Ives to Balmoral, but in 1972 Kim was enrolled at Abbotsleigh, much closer to home, and in 1973 Robyn joined the Abbotsleigh staff as second Deputy.[2]

Abbotsleigh was and is still one of Sydney's leading private girls' schools, with historical stately buildings and a top academic reputation. Robyn was glad to do what her mother had done before her and through her work paid for Kim's school fees. But it was the kind of work that Robyn loved. "Teaching was in my blood," she said later. In fact she loved it so much that she would have taught there without being paid if she hadn't needed the money!

The school loved her too, and, after eight years as the second Deputy, Robyn became the Vice Principal. It was just as well she was an energetic person because she took on a vast array of responsibilities.

First and foremost was her teaching. Robyn had a knack for making lessons come alive through imaginative presentation. Girls were always eager to join her classes, and she paid attention to both the gifted and the less gifted students. Her knowledge of the subject and style of teaching gained her respect, but she wasn't above having

---

[1] Miss V. Medway, Headmistress of Queenwood, said in her history of Queenwood, that Robyn contributed significantly to the "feel of the school and to its scholarship."

[2] Known then as First Assistant.

the odd prank pulled on her. All teachers develop certain habits that they are mostly unaware of, and, for several years, Robyn had ended her classes when the bell went by shutting her book firmly and saying, "That's that". She was extremely surprised and amused one day when she heard the bell to see her 25 students bang their books closed and say in unison, "That's that."

School policy kept teachers from having their own children in their classes, so Robyn never taught Kim until she was in Year 11 and the system for senior English had changed. The girls were now allowed to choose from several different topics, and Robyn was delighted when Kim ended up in her classes for a few weeks. Kim found it hard to call Robyn, 'Mrs Claydon' like everyone else. 'Mother' came to her much more readily. After a few lessons, the Year 11 girls started to address their questions to 'Mother' as well!

Robyn loved teaching English, but she didn't separate the subject from the students. She was able to relate her teaching to their lives, and help them learn real lessons from the topic. One student was inspired to go into teaching because of the way Robyn "used her teaching so meaningfully as a method of nurturing and developing individuals". She wrote: "It showed me a new dimension to using our professions and how God blesses those who are faithful in using their gifts for him."[3]

This ability to relate to the girls gave her another role as a counsellor in the school. It was just like 'Juvenile Jury' all over again, except this time Robyn had a lot more experience and wisdom.

Once a girl came to her worried that she was pregnant. Robyn took her to her own doctor for a test, which happily turned out to be negative.

"Can you imagine the consequences if the results had been positive?" Robyn said to her after the girl got over her relief. "I would

---

[3] Gail Pilley, an ex-Abbotsleigh student, wrote in 1987 to say how she had been inspired by Robyn.

have had to ring your parents. You might have had to leave school."

The student took Robyn seriously, and visited her frequently for advice and counsel after that. Many other girls brought their problems to Robyn's office, and she seemed always to have time for them, no matter 'how silly or trivial they seemed'.[4] Her patience, ability to perceive underlying issues, and understanding of the need to listen first stood her in good stead, and parents and girls respected her for the way she dealt with problems with fairness, consideration and sensitivity.

As in most cases, the older you get, the more you understand, and Robyn wishes now that she had been wiser or more knowledgeable in some areas of counselling. However, for the most part, her efforts were well appreciated, even by other staff, who wrote a song for her birthday one year:

'How do you solve a problem? Just ask Robyn!

Who do you call on when you're feeling blue?

Where do you take your whinges and your grumbles?

Just open the staffroom door and join the queue!'[5]

As well as counselling, Robyn also had the job of dealing with any discipline problems that came up. This was not usually a major problem as Abbotsleigh girls were from families that valued education. Robyn was able to put more of her time into pioneering and teaching the school's Personal Development (PD) program.

PD aimed to help the girls grow in maturity, to learn how to make good choices and to develop their self-esteem and their capacity to reach their potential. Robyn took the girls through a series of 'uplifting' talks and exercises on things like honest self-analysis, overcoming failure, confidence and peer pressure. The PD program became a successful part of the school's pastoral care for

---

[4] Student Melanie Duncan wrote an essay about Robyn entitled, "Someone I will always remember". She said that Robyn would always answer troubles in a helpful way: no matter how silly or trivial they sounded, she always had an excellent answer.

[5] To the tune of 'How do you solve a problem like Maria?'

students. Robyn wrote an interactive textbook on the subject, and visited America in 1983 to further her experience in the area.

All of Madelon's training and mentoring were bearing fruit in Robyn's career. Her abilities to communicate and speak in public were well used in chapel services. The school chaplain was gracious enough to call her 'one of the most inspiring preachers I have heard'.[6] She could draw pictures in people's minds, and use common objects or situations as learning tools.

One image that is remembered by many Abbotsleigh old girls was Robyn's use of her hand to explain that 'everybody is a *thumb*body'. It might have been overly cute for any slightly cynical teenagers at the time, but it was still making its point years later!

Robyn approached everybody in the same positive way. She seemed to have boundless energy, and was constantly vivacious and cheerful. This relentless vitality was not always appreciated by some of the more melancholy students, but it was never 'put on' by Robyn, and it earned her the genuine love and respect of most people associated with the school. One parent said that she had a ready smile, and a way of relaxing even the most uptight person.[7] Student Melanie Duncan likened her to being both 'one of the girls' as well as 'a second mother.'

Robyn used both personas to make her point with wit, flair and often, verse. To help the girls understand why they should listen in chapel, she penned this ditty:

Ten little Abbotsleigh girls thought they were divine,

One came in late for chapel and then there were nine.

Nine little Abbotsleigh girls waited for the plate,

One let it go right past and then there were eight.

Eight little Abbotsleigh girls thought they were heading for heaven,

---

[6] Rev RF McDonald, Chaplain of Abbotsleigh
[7] Dawn Anderson, Abbotsleigh parent, in 1986

One played with a Rubics cube and then there were seven.
Seven little Abbotsleigh girls knew that chapel and talking don't mix,
One didn't kneel in prayer and then there were six.
Six little Abbotsleigh girls towards goodness decided to strive,
One nodded off in the sermon, and then there were five.
Five little Abbotsleigh girls were eager to hear some more,
One read a book instead and then there were four.
Four little Abbotsleigh girls sang the hymns with glee,
One folded all the pages and then there were three.
Three little Abbotsleigh girls – now getting rather few,
One didn't come at all, and then there were two.
Two little Abbotsleigh girls heard of Christ, God's Son,
One didn't even listen, and then there was one.
One little Abbotsleigh girl sat and listened and prayed,
And when the service was over, she was glad that she had stayed.

She also used her personal experiences to teach and encourage. In 1988, after a short illness, Robyn's beloved father Ronald Hickin passed away at the age of 76. Robyn had the privilege of conducting his funeral service. At assembly that week she shared with the girls not only her sadness, but also her peace and hope of knowing he was now in heaven with the Lord. Many of the girls were touched, and one wrote to thank Robyn;

"Mrs Claydon, I wonder if you realise the impact you made on so many girls in Friday's Assembly? They marvelled at your courage and peace of mind, and I believe it made many think seriously about Christianity. Thank you so much... You are a fine example to us all."[8]

If there was one thing that Robyn dearly wanted to get across to the students, it was that her Christian faith was real; it made a massive difference in her own life, and it should be considered seriously by every girl for herself. Students, staff and parents could

[8] Letter from school girl Linda Morris, May 1988.

see this clearly. One parent said, "It is obvious to all who know her that Jesus does indeed walk with her in her journey through life."[9]

And for a student to write that the greatest impact she had was her "joyful Christian witness and her constant striving to provide new opportunities for both individual girls and the school as a whole"[10] would have been all that Robyn would have wanted to achieve.

Robyn was fortunate indeed. She was enjoying the opportunity to use her talents and to do what she loved to great effect and to great applause. She was respected and loved in her community. She had managed to combine this with being a mother and a supporter-wife of a man who was similarly gifted and active. And she had reached, almost without trying, a level of Christian joy and maturity that others struggle for their entire lives.

Even her family, and families always know best, acknowledged that Robyn's Christian life was completely genuine. Her sister wrote later: "Some Christians seem to come calmly to such a stage of maturity; others of us lurch there, through much pain…. It seems to me my sister has managed to do the former."[11]

While life at school was busy, life at home was no less so. As Kim grew up, Robyn took the opportunity to continue her studies. Her academic qualifications were gained the 'hard way' – studying at night and on weekends, while working full time and looking after her home.

David had also kept up his schedule of being away frequently. As General Secretary, these trips were made around the State, but as Federal Secretary and while working in the South Pacific, he began to travel overseas more often.

In 1979 he went to Singapore for Scripture Union's Asia-Pacific

---

[9] Dr Thomas W Anderson, Abbotsleigh parent, 1986

[10] Gail Pilley, student in 1987

[11] Marlene Hickin (Cohen) in her book *The Divided Self*, 1996 Harper Collins, Great Britain

Robyn conducting the Abbotsleigh Centenary Pageant, 1985

Kim & David on their wedding day at St Matthew's, 1987

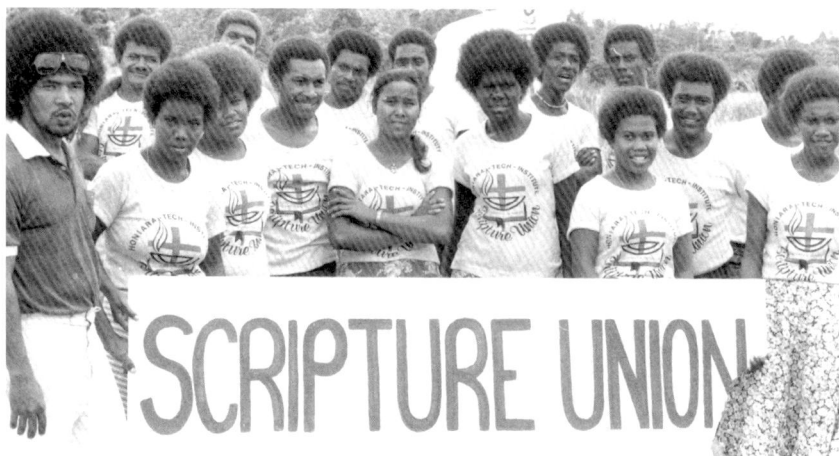

First SU Camp in Solomons, 1973, led by David

Robyn's Lausanne Young Women's Mentoring Group meeting in Berlin

Sketch of St Matthew's, West Pennant Hills

Lausanne South Pacific Women's 1993 Conference

Robyn with Vera Izotova, Moscow

Robyn with a Zulu evangelist (a tribal princess)

*David with Dr John Azumah of Ghana first non-Australian to
be appointed a missionary by CMS Australia*

Tanzanian pastor receiving gift of bicycle from David on behalf of CMS

David with youth at the newly planted church in Phnom Penh, Cambodia

All Saints Cathedral, Cairo, where David is a Canon

David with grandchildren: Andrew & Georgia

Kim, David, Andrew and Georgia Barker

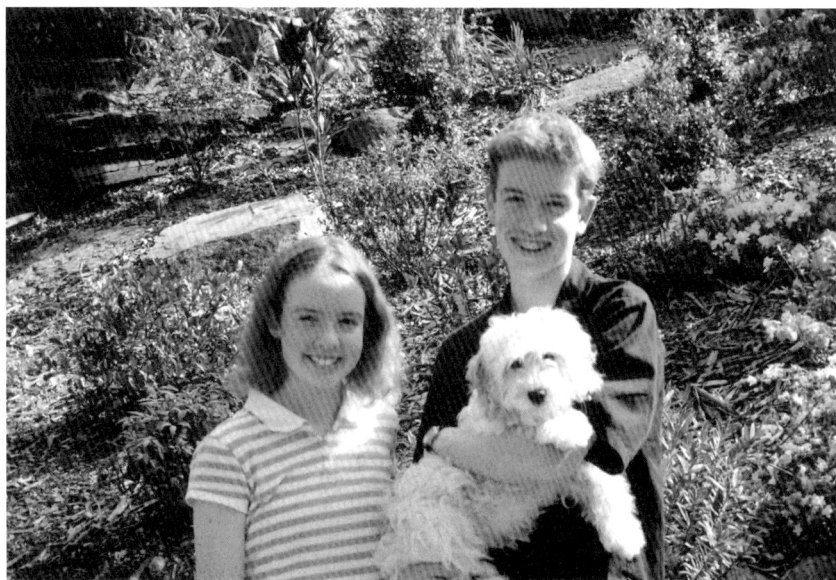
Georgia & Andrew with their much loved spoodle, Mia, 2004

ANZEA Regional Council meeting to help in staff-training and policy setting. Then it was on to London for talks on Bible reading materials, and after that to Edinburgh for an SU International Council meeting.

Despite his travels, he remained close to his two girls, who badly wanted to go with him! When David visited the famous Raffles hotel in Singapore, Robyn told him to "enjoy it and look around with three sets of eyes." He always did, and wrote back long detailed letters with descriptions of places and people to amuse them.

Kim sent letters to amuse him too. On his 1979 trip, she made a game for him to play on the plane. She wrote, tongue in cheek, "I hope this will not prove to be too mentally taxing on you." He was sent off with specific jobs to do for her too, including looking for tennis books, getting popular Christian singer Evie's autograph and collecting airline stickers.

In the days when inflight movies were still very novel and exciting, Kim was very jealous that David was able to watch a new film on the plane that had not yet come out in Australia. Unfortunately, David wasn't quite as aware of his luck! He watched the film with one eye on the screen, the other eye on his paper on the problems with liberation theology, and the inflight classical music channel playing through his headphones. But he still wrote to Kim to tell her that Farrah Fawcett was in the film. "I knew it was she because someone told me!"

Other big trips included the International Prayer Assembly in Korea in 1984. This conference was designed to follow up Lausanne 1974 by having deep and committed prayer for World Evangelism. In true Korean praying style, the prayer sessions were to David's ears "an incredible cacophony of sound". Although he found the teaching weak, the prayer obviously moved him, and he came back determined to promote prayer in the Australia Pacific region.

A year later, in 1985, he attended the International Scripture

Union Conference held in Zimbabwe, with 350 delegates from 50 countries. David wrote, "The tremendous spirit and fellowship was indicative of the presence of God's Holy Spirit amongst us all".

On some of his overseas travels, Robyn and Kim were able to come too, and the family enjoyed quite a number of international holidays at the end of conferences. More often than not, however, David was away by himself, missing his family badly in the few spare minutes he allowed himself in each busy day.

He wrote things like, "My loving thanks to both of you for putting up with my absences," and "I keep thinking all the day as to what you're both doing."

Sometimes what they were doing were just the things of everyday life, but sometimes David missed special occasions. Sadly, he was away when Robyn graduated with her MA. He wrote that day, "I thought about you until I went to sleep."

Other special occasions that he missed frequently were the annual school plays. Kim would write in great detail about them, and one year threatened him with, "You'd better make sure that you're home for it next time!"

Thankfully, he got home for the very special production of 1985.

Abbotsleigh School had reached its centenary in 1985, and Robyn, who was so keen to promote school spirit that she always had her entire office hung in the school colours of black and gold, used her musical and dramatic abilities to write an eight-scene pageant of the school's history.

Robyn had written large, colourful pageants before for school events, but this was extra-special.[12] Every student had a part in it and it would be the crowning event in a week-long series of celebrations and commemorations.

---

[12] The closing song of the 90th birthday pageant, which Robyn wrote for Abbotsleigh in 1975, became the school song. Later, Robyn's granddaughter Georgia would be able to sing it even before she started at Abbotsleigh.

The planning went on for months, and the girls' excitement was building. At one assembly, all the girls were told that they would have to dress in period costume for the whole centenary week. The next week at assembly, Robyn and Miss Kathleen McCredie, the headmistress, paraded on stage in their own period dresses and parasols. The girls roared as their two head teachers daintily modelled their gowns.

The week of festivities was well received, and the pageant was a resounding success with girls, parents and staff. One teacher said that the greatest benefit for her was the improved relationships with the girls throughout the preparation. A parent commented not only on the professional presentation, and its smooth running, but on "the total enthusiasm of everyone on the night. Every eye was shining with delight just to be part of such a momentous celebration."[13]

Robyn's gifts and energy didn't go unnoticed by the school community, and some wondered how she managed to keep it all together. One even wrote to find out: "How you constantly give your 'all' for the school and for the girls I do not know, but to end on a somewhat lighter note, may I ask, 'Do you go home and kick the cat?' "[14]

The Claydons did have a cat. But it certainly wasn't kicked. Robyn was extremely blessed to have energy, good health, an easy-going family and a faith in God which sustained her through everything. She would need all of these as she and David took a new turn into parish ministry.

[13] Roz Lloyd-Phillips, in a letter in 1985.
[14] Patti Garrity – parent. Letter in 1985

Chapter Seventeen

Set sail for the South Pacific!

Scripture Union in Australia had its various challenges, but it was nothing like the challenges in Asia. In Thailand, for example, a tiny number of local believers lived in a culture where there was no encouragement for reading, almost no books and no words for 'God' or 'sin'.

In Thailand, one missionary returning after furlough found that almost all his hard-won converts had returned to Buddhism. He asked one of the older Christians why this was. "You gave us a church and a faith, but you never taught us how to study the Bible," the old man said.

The missionary contacted Scripture Union, which had only just appointed a Thai staff person, and asked them to produce Thai Bible reading notes with study questions. In a year, circulation was up to 1000.

David Chan, based in Singapore and in charge of the SU East Asia-Pacific Region (known as ANZEA) with over one third of the world's population living in his area, had his hands extremely full. So, in 1977, David Claydon was asked to give him some help. While continuing as Australian Federal Secretary, he would take on the SU ministry in the South Pacific.

In contrast to Asia's teeming millions, his new area of ministry covered half the world's oceans, but a total population of only 21 million, including Australia and New Zealand.

"The Pacific Islands are easy to discount; they have no influence in world affairs, and, in some parts, life is primitive. But before God, everyone matters," he wrote to praying friends as he began.

There were seven English-speaking and three French-speaking

significant Pacific Island nations where a church was established. Scripture Union was already functioning in some of these, and they could see the need to minister in the others. A major challenge would be nominalism. In the New Hebrides[1], 73 per cent of the tiny population of 103,000 called themselves Christian, but, as in most of the islands, there was little Christian activity apart from traditional church programs. David found a wide open door for both Scripture Union's Bible reading ministry and its work in schools.[2]

Working in the laid-back Pacific couldn't be done from behind a desk in fast-paced, clock-watching Sydney. David would have to visit, and seriously adjust his life-style.

David's natural organisational tendency was to use every minute to good purpose. He frequently used his air travel time to write papers or answer letters. He never 'wasted' a lunch time eating sandwiches by himself if he could meet someone useful to talk with. Once on an overseas trip, stopping at a seminary graduation in Taiwan on the invitation of a friend, he found the whole ceremony was in Taiwanese, which he didn't understand. Instead of sitting and not comprehending, he used the time to surreptitiously write to Robyn and Kim.

To find himself in the Pacific, in a culture with a remarkably different use of time and a very laissez-faire attitude, was at first a little bit of a shock. "Working in the Pacific is extremely demanding of one's patience, and requires a real sense of dependence on God and yet hard work," he wrote to prayer supporters.

The first visit to each of the Islands was probably the most difficult. He didn't know anyone, he didn't know where he would be staying, and he didn't even know if he would be met at the airport.

This was the case when he arrived on one of the smaller New Hebrides islands. Landing on a grass air-strip, he saw no-one waving

[1] Now Vanuatu.
[2] *God's Word in a Young World* Nigel Sylvester 1984 p 206

helpfully to him. The Cessna pilot assured him that this was the right island. David sat under a palm tree reading his book and praying that someone would turn up. After an hour a man with a machete appeared. He said that he was the person who cut the grass on the airstrip. David explained that he was supposed to be going to the theological college, so the man told David to follow him. They walked some two kilometres through the bush and came to a bay. The grass-cutter said that the College always sent a boat to pick up its guests and the boat should be here. They pushed through the bush and walked through the low tide corals around a point where they could see a cruiser out in the bay.

"That's the mission boat. But the fellows have gone walk-about and should be here soon," said David's new friend.

So David waited. When the men from the boat finally arrived back, they all boarded the tiny mooring boat nearby and rowed out, bailing frantically as they went; the rowboat had no plug in its drain hole!

Finally on the cruiser, as it was cranked up, he looked into the clear blue water below to see the beautiful sight of bright blue, yellow and striped coral fish lit up by the rays of the sun. When they arrived at their destination, it was back into the leaky rowboat until it was grounded on the coral, and then he took off his shoes and walked through the shallows to his destination. The shoes stayed off for the remainder of his stay.

Changing time zones did eventually become easier. Bill Andersen remembers David getting on the plane in Sydney, up to his ears in issues, policy, administration and time management. When the plane landed, he was able to get out, relaxed and ready to go at the Islander pace.

Part of getting to know the Island culture meant staying with local pastors and leaders in their homes. This was often less relaxing than it seemed. On one trip, David had returned early and alone to his host's house one night. He went inside and was looking for a place to sit by the light of the single lantern on the floor, when he saw what seemed to be a large bean bag in one corner of the large room. It looked comfortable and inviting, but it was lucky he decided to sit on the floor in the usual style. When the men arrived back from the church, the 'bean bag' – the pastor's ample wife - turned over and yelled out to a daughter to bring some tea for the guests.

Tea was fine, but eating the rich islander food was not something David ever really enjoyed. He could smell the coconut coming out of his pores, and, after five or six days of being polite and eating all that was offered, he found himself dreaming at night of getting on the plane to eat something he could enjoy.

Despite the challenges, David's special joy was to find himself so very quickly part of God's family in a completely new culture, with people he had never met and situations he had never encountered before. "It was quite beyond my imagination how many factors came together to enable me to be able to extend the work of SU in the Pacific," he wrote in his diary on his first trip.

And the work was being extended. The first visits were used for looking at the local situation, making contacts and talking with almost everybody he could find. Church leaders of all denominations were on his list of people to meet. School principals and local teachers were also priorities. Talking, listening, asking questions, observing and noting were part of the strategy, and David made copious notes every night, even down to the details of his hosts' children's names and ages.

On subsequent visits he would get back in touch with his contacts and try to set up an SU committee of enthusiastic people, look for staff who would be well-accepted locally, and then encourage them, help them work out how to be self-supporting and sort through any problems with them.[3]

[3] *Lighting the Lamp* by John and Moyra Prince 1980

Of course there were problems. As in any place, difficulties in personality, political power plays and splits and divisions reared their head from time to time. The hardest thing was to get the support for SU from within the culture, instead of imposing it from the outside. In some areas, SU was seen as a threat to the local church. David's answer to this was to try to find the right people to take on the work - highly regarded locals with ability and enthusiasm. After that, they had to set up structures that would work *for* the people, the churches and Scripture Union, instead of against them.

This was not as easy as it seemed. On his first visit to Tonga, David found a healthy Scripture Union interacting well with local churches because of a dynamic Tongan committee chairman. A thousand people attended the SU camp every year, and the circulation of SU Bible reading notes was said to be greater than the daily newspaper.

Within two years, the popular leader had shifted his theological position, had launched an attack on the Wesleyan church and the government, and had tried to organise SU into a separate church. Unsurprisingly, church leaders lost confidence and the work collapsed.[4]

David's need for combining strategy and prayerfulness had never been greater. He relied heavily on the prayers of Scripture Union staff and supporters, but also on a group of more personal supporters who received his prayer letters. His prayer requests were many and varied: "I need your prayers for wisdom as I work out how to establish a truly national ministry which helps the church in its work."

"Some time in July/August I need to visit Fiji, New Hebrides, Tonga and Samoa. However, I can't get an answer out of the Samoan translator, and I need to land in the New Hebrides at a time which

[4] *God's Word in a Young World* Nigel Sylvester 1984 p 206

avoids the major political strife which is about to burst out. Then Tonga want me to be at their large evangelistic camp at a time which doesn't easily fit the other spots - so please pray for me as I work out my movements. I am utterly dependent on God's guidance in choosing the right dates for some unpredictable situations."

The prayers of these faithful praying people were answered by God in wonderful ways. After his first trip, David wrote in his journal: "I have seen God in action in my life in many and marvellous ways, but I can't recall a three-week period like this when I have seen God go before me, lead, direct, give me the words to speak, the right questions to ask and the encouragement of results in such a continuous way. I just praise God for all this and pray that I will see the plans and promises come to fruition."

In 1978 he wrote, reporting back to the praying supporters, "Again I saw God at work in such a remarkable way that at times my body tingled all over!"

Prayers from others and his own hurried requests to God for his 'leading and energy' were his source of strength through the minutes of each day. Many times he would pray about a problem, and then find the answer in a person who was already on the way to meet him as he prayed.

On one trip, after spending all day talking with people, he lost his voice and did not know how he was going to stand up and give a message to yet another group. "I had prayed that somehow I could raise more than a whisper... when I opened my mouth quite a strong voice came out! So I praised God in my heart as I went on speaking."

Losing his voice was not very surprising, given that most days David was up at 6am and not in bed before 11pm, and often later. Even though the pace of life was different, he was working hard, speaking, travelling, learning and listening.

He was also put on the spot frequently, and given only a few minutes notice to speak or present a Bible study to different groups.

At one Scripture Union get-together, David was planning to speak from Acts 4, but when he got there he found the audience was made up of children, not high-schoolers as he had thought. The talk was quickly changed to the story of King Josiah.

After many visits, some challenges and much prayer, by the end of 1983 the ministry had grown. Scripture Union was now working in seven Island nations. In five of these there was an SU ministry in most of the secondary schools. In all seven a Bible reading ministry was doing well. In the smaller nations, SU was the only interdenominational outreach ministry.

"So we have a great responsibility and praise God for the encouragement of seeing wonderful results," David wrote.

And the results in people's lives were wonderful. In 1980 the number of conversions amongst high school students in the Solomon Islands had been so remarkable that school principals commented to David on the complete change in the atmosphere of their schools.

At a camp in Fiji, David shared a room with a teacher who had been converted only three years before at university. As a violent, hard drinker, his conversion had come as a bit of a shock to the student body. Now a teacher, the young man was running the ISCF at Fiji's school for chiefs' sons, with tremendous impact.

God was working in people's lives in the South Pacific, but he was also moving in David's life. By 1980, David had been working with Scripture Union for 21 good years, but his thoughts and desire were stirring in different directions. It was time to move on.

After so many years leading Scripture Union, the words of farewell he was given were both warm and glowing.

Alan Kerr commented on his 'calm competence and unusual combination of gifts[5]'. The SU Council[6] mentioned his 'theological

[5] Alan Kerr – on farewell from SU Australian Council 1980
[6] Minute of appreciation by Australian Council of SU, 26-28 Sept 1980

146

gifts, pastoral gifts, gifts of public ministry, analytical gifts, organisational gifts and economic and accountancy gifts'.

David had played a central role in developing a national consciousness and identity, establishing goals and raising standards. It was an 'an exacting job well done' by a person who had an 'obvious knowledge of and love for the Lord', a 'warm interest in people' and a 'visionary mind that can also grapple with practical realities'[7].

David was sad to leave. But God had plans to use his gifts in a new area altogether. David was going to get ordained.

---

[7] Tasmania SU publication Nov 1980

CHAPTER EIGHTEEN

LAUSANNE 74 AND A NEW DIRECTION

Kairos and the Jesus people movement had seemed to tap into the mood of young people of the day so well in the mid-1970s that, by comparison, David felt the established church was becoming more and more irrelevant to the rising generation.

Frankly, he thought church services were boring. Most preachers he had heard he found to be uninteresting, and he had not yet been in a church with a warm sense of fellowship. In fact, he had felt this way since he was a teenager, even though he had attended at least two services a week since he was 12 and had brought his friends along as well.

As a child and a teenager, David went to church because whoever he was living with at the time thought he should. Lora took him from the time he lived with her. He went weekly with the Politians in Jerusalem. He had to go at boarding school and he even went while he was living at the guest house!

The guest house owners, the Bartrops, were Brethren. They only went to one service a Sunday themselves, but they were concerned that David wasn't attending the local Anglican evening services as well as the morning. They kindly rang his rector, who encouraged him to come in the evenings as well by asking him to give the Bible readings at night. David agreed to go because it was unusual for a layperson in those days to read the Bible in the services and he was happy to do this.

But he was also disillusioned with church structures. He had always expected that the church leadership would speak to and challenge the community on current issues, much like he was trying to do at SU, but he could not see it happening. "It shouldn't be this way, should it?" he asked himself.

Part of the problem was that nobody had ever told him why people went to church. In fact, attending church seemed to be the missing 11th Commandment: if a Christian meeting is on, thou shalt go.

Remarkably, David's faith in God and love for Christ were strong and thriving, despite his ambivalence towards church. And the Jesus movement brought into sharp focus for him the fact that other young people were growing in Christ outside the institutional church.

The questions burning in his head were "What is so important about church?" and "Can the church possibly survive?"

The second thing that the Jesus movement brought into sharp perspective for him was that young people outside the church were really thinking about what it meant for them to be Christians in a secular world. The word 'radical' was well-used amongst the Jesus people, and it was making him question what it meant to be a radical follower of Christ.

In an interview in the early 1970s, David admitted, "I really do not feel that the committed Christians within the church are really radical towards life. They have become contained within the system..."

"We know that the whole concept of becoming a Christian is that there is this radical change in your life. But it's not just a radical change in your relationship with God. It is also a radical change in your relationship with each other and towards society.... "

"If our young people were really turned on to be radical in their thinking, then I believe we'd be attracting a lot more young people in to the church who want to think that way... The church ought to be leading the way.[1]"

---

[1] Interview published in *On the Move* magazine August 1974

With these questions and doubts playing large in his mind, it was just as well David was invited to Lausanne 1974.[2] This would be a meeting that would change his thinking and shape the course of his life to come.

The International Congress on World Evangelization was held in Lausanne, Switzerland, in 1974. It was a global leadership conference on reaching the world for Christ, sponsored by the Billy Graham organization. More than 2,300 evangelists and Christian leaders from 150 different countries around the world were invited to attend, to share their experiences, and to think together about the world-wide task of evangelism still ahead. The gathering produced the 'Lausanne Covenant', a declaration that was 'intended to define the necessity, responsibilities and goals of spreading the gospel'.[3]

David was invited to Lausanne 1974 because of his Scripture Union role, and was asked to speak about 'Holiday and Beach evangelism' in a ninety-minute session. It turned out to be a 'worthwhile and practical' hour and a half, but it was what he gained from Lausanne, not what he gave to it, that would change him.

The first issue he was able to work on was what it meant to be truly a radical follower of Christ.

Frequently, evangelicals have regarded evangelism - speaking the good news of the gospel of Christ - and social concern as mutually exclusive. And the hotly debated theological issue of Lausanne 1974 was precisely the relationship of evangelism and social justice.

David and a few others, including the Australian Baptist minister John Hirt and Os Guinness, a staff member of L'Abri , set up a 'radical discipleship' study group.

<hr />

[2] David had been a plenary speaker at the Asia South Pacific Congress on Evangelism (organised by the Billy Graham Association) held in Singapore in 1968.

[3] C Rene Padilla asserts that Lausanne 1974 was the most important worldwide evangelical gathering of the 20th century. It became a catalyst for evangelism and a matrix for theological reflection on issues that were placed on the evangelical missionary agenda by the Lausanne Covenant. Ref his paper on Integral Mission and its Historical Development, presented at the Micah Network Conference, Oxford 2001. www.micahchallenge.org

Deeply concerned that what was written in the draft covenant did not reflect what had been said in the plenary sessions about evangelism and the inherent challenge to societal needs, the Radical Discipleship group wrote to the drafting committee with an alternative statement.

This paper was called 'A Response to Lausanne', and included statements such as:

"There is no biblical dichotomy between the word spoken and the word made visible in the lives of God's people. Men will look as they listen and what they see must be at one with what they hear."

"There are times when our communication may be by attitude and action only, and times when the spoken word will stand alone; but we must repudiate as demonic the attempt to drive a wedge between evangelism and social action."

"Those who proclaim the cross must be continually marked by the cross."

"With unashamed commitment to Jesus Christ, we must engage in the mutual listening of dialogue, the reward of which is understanding."

The paper was long, challenging and strong, and was written "with a sense of repentance towards the Lord for failure in fully grasping this issue, and with a sense of appreciation for the opportunity of a Congress like this which has so challenged us in this area."[4] The Lausanne Congress Planning Committee allowed the Radical Discipleship Group to call an ad hoc meeting of those who shared these concerns.[5] Some 800 young Lausanne participants from all corners of the world gathered, and, under David's chairmanship, they developed a new paragraph for the covenant which Dr John Stott very ably edited and added to the Covenant as clause 5.

These discussions confirmed David's belief that Christians must be Christian not just in words alone, but in deeds also. The church

---

[4] Memo to the committee drafting the Congress Covenant. (J.D.Douglas, *ed Let the Earth Hear His Voice: Official Reference Volume,* World Wide Publications, 1975, p1294-96)

[5] Church Scene, 15 August 1974

had to demonstrate to the society around it the reality and the difference of being members of God's covenanted community. He now saw the call to discipleship as a call to both proclaim the gospel of Jesus Christ, and to work for reconciliation amongst people.[6]

The second major thing David gained from the conference was a new appreciation for the church.

The issue of whether the church could survive was addressed by Michael Griffiths and Paul Snyder. They brought out truths that David had probably always known, but never really appreciated. The church is God's calling and made up of God's people! No matter what the problems with it, God is not going to let go his hold of it. Because it is Christ's presence on earth, it will survive.

Up to this point, David had thought that 'church' included the denomination and the structures as well as the gathering of God's people, instead of seeing that the local fellowship and not the structures are 'church'. Now he could see that the denominational superstructure is 'parachurch', or a sort of add-on. David could see it was needed to manage the affairs of the fellowship, to build in checks and balances and to make pastors accountable. The fact that the structures may be ungainly or bureaucratic, in the end doesn't affect the local fellowship of believers gathering together to learn from God's word and to give him praise.

David came back from Lausanne with a completely refreshed, almost new understanding of what it meant to be church. And rather than looking to get out of it, he began to think about his own contribution inside it. Even though he was a confirmed member of the Anglican church, he had not often been enthusiastically involved – up until now.[7]

---

[6] As he shared with Brisbane clergy at a lunch time meeting on Feb 6, 1974.

[7] At around this time David was elected by Synod to be a member of the Moore College Committee. With the Lausanne experience he accepted the invitation and continued on the Committee until he became Rector of St Matthew's, West Pennant Hills

David and Robyn attended Christ Church St Ives, where Dudley Foord was the rector. Foord was bringing a freshness to services that David appreciated through contemporary music and the involvement of lay people. Members of the congregation were asked to lead the prayers, give testimonies, or answer questions about their lives and ministries. This was novel and innovative – and David liked it.

"There are other ways to do things," he thought to himself. "Perhaps I could contribute to this. But what can I do as a normal church member?"

David could see that lay people could have a great impact on their neighbours and their work colleagues, as they lived out and spoke about the gospel of Christ in their day to day lives. But it was clear to him that, in the public arena of media and law making, only the leadership in the church ever had the opportunity to speak and to be heard.

This brought him to another thought: "Perhaps I should get ordained."

It was time, with Robyn, to seek God's guidance, to think and to pray about a new direction in life. Driving home one day, David felt God spoke to him very clearly, that he should move on and be ordained.

All the logical signs seemed to be pointing that way; twenty-one years in Scripture Union seemed long enough. And the only way to develop a broad range of preaching[8] or pastoral skills seemed to be by being ordained and becoming involved in parish ministry.

Affirmation by trusted friends and family seemed to confirm the call too. David discussed it with Bishop John Reid who encouraged him to proceed, and Robyn was delighted as she had always thought she would marry a clergyman!

---

[8] David did preach with SU, but the topic was usually related to Bible reading or something similar.

Lora too was thrilled and gave him a 'travelling communion set': a silver cup and plate to take when he visited the sick and infirm.[9]

Although David had worked with church leaders of many different denominations in his time at Scripture Union, he decided to seek ordination in the Anglican church. Family ties certainly played a part in this – the Claydons, the Hickins and the Arrowsmiths were Anglicans, but he could see other advantages too. The Anglican Church's formularies are biblical, the Sydney diocese is evangelical and non-ritualistic, and Anglicans are widely accepted by the whole community, making neighbourhood evangelism much easier.

David would have made an excellent poker player; he still played his cards very close to his chest. And he took a lot of his friends by surprise when he announced his ordination in a casual second paragraph in one of his regular prayer letters in 1979.

"This year there will be a slight change of life-style on Sundays..." he wrote.

One friend sent back a fast reply: "It was a great surprise to us both to read of your plans," and another said, "Honest! When I was speaking to you the other day I didn't know. But the power of the media and the grapevine has brought me up to date."

Even Bruce Upton, one of his closest friends, was taken aback, "given our many conversations on the matter over the past 15 years!"

But despite the surprise, there was affirmation. "You have a gift that 'church' folk need today," wrote Keith Frazer.[10] "By that I mean you convey to people that, when their life is yielded to God as Lord and Saviour, Christianity becomes a real and vital way of life

---

[9] Lora was delighted with this because her father, Ernest Claydon, had been an Anglican clergyman. In fact, Lora was always hoping that David would become a Canon like her father. Unfortunately she passed away before it happened.

[10] Then chair of the Newcastle, NSW Scripture Union Regional Committee

in business, home, children, sport etc. ie. a practical way of life, seven days per week."

There was also some timely advice. Dr Paul White, David's mentor and advisor from university days, wrote: "I've followed your doings since you were a boy and prayed for you, and, at stages, pushed your barrow a little. Avoid the vinegar club and don't let the enemy sell you any side tracks."

David was deaconed and priested in 1979 at St Andrew's Cathedral in Sydney. It was a direction that would affect not just him, but the whole of the Claydon family, as they all became more involved in the new ministry.

CHAPTER NINETEEN

INTO THE PARISH

The transition from Scripture Union to parish life was gradual for David, Robyn and Kim. In 1979, David became the honorary curate at St Swithun's, Pymble, working with the warm and supportive Bishop Clive Kerle on Sundays, and keeping up with his SU Federal Secretary job during the week. But no-one could help noticing that the 'Claydon Trio', as Kerle dubbed them, plunged themselves wholeheartedly into the parish.

1981 turned out to be another year when David and Robyn could 'practise' ministry. David was Acting Rector of St Alban's, Lindfield, and the family continued to live at their St Ives home.

It was a good but challenging experience, with a heavy teaching load each week, a number of special events to organize, and some draining pastoral work with the sudden accidental death of a 10 year old boy in one of the church families. Robyn and David again worked together ministering to their congregation.

But, in 1982, David was invited to be the rector of St Matthew's, West Pennant Hills.

St Matthew's was a flourishing church[1] in one of Sydney's newer suburbs, with plenty of young families in the area. The church had a modern new building, a great outreach and mission focus, a good track record of pastoral care, and, somewhat surprisingly for many Australian churches, a very strong and involved contingent of committed Christian men.[2]

And the church knew what it was looking for. When David first read their job description, he thought it was 'really most

---

[1] St Matthew's had quite a sizeable congregation. In 1983 the average total attendance on Sundays was 380 adults and 100 or so children and teens.

[2] *A history of St Matthew's Anglican Church* by Judy Taylor, 1996.

challenging'. They wanted a rector who was an able preacher, but also someone who could enthuse the congregation in evangelism. He had to be a warm pastor as well. And it wouldn't hurt to have a wife who was keen on parish life. He also must be personally involved in mission!

According to the group of parish nominators who chose him, he and Robyn fitted the bill. They responded very warmly to his involvement in the SU Pacific work, and gave him permission to be away from the parish for three weeks a year (apart from holidays) to continue it.

So from February 1982, the Claydons moved into the rectory in West Pennant Hills, and began their ministry at the affectionately dubbed 'St Matt's'.[3]

David's first concern came from his years of thinking about church and its problems. St Matthew's was already an active church, with many able people who wanted to serve the Lord, but David wanted it to go even further. He wanted to know how they could together build a body of people who love Christ, and, because of their love for Jesus, love each other. And, practically, how could the people of the church really genuinely show that they loved each other.

He began to pray and talk with key people straight away about the theological basis for everything the church did and wanted to do. Out of these discussions, they began to set goals and plans and present them to the church.

The first four sermons that David preached at St Matthew's were about church: what it was, what it meant, and how it could work.

The big innovation to get things going was the system of Parish Fellowship Groups. The PFGs were a network of neighbourhood

---

[3] Moving was the hardest for Kim, who had lived in the same house practically all her life and had just finished school. In the end, she conceded that she enjoyed it: she made plenty of friends at St Matthew's, and even met her husband, David Barker, there.

groups, originally set up on a geographical basis. They would be for Bible study, pastoral care and welcoming newcomers, and would be the basis for each person in the church to have a strong identity and to share in ministry.

The idea seems obvious today, but it was still new in 1982. By the end of the year, between 70 and 80 percent of adults had voluntarily joined a group, and the positive repercussions of this new system of Bible study and pastoral caring were flowing over into the wider congregation.

St Matthew's as a church was keen to share the gospel in their neighbourhood, so an Outreach Council was set up to help in this. By the end of 1982, men's dinners and film and study series had been started to reach out. The fellowship groups were also helpful in outreach. In 1984 they held a 'Hospitality Week', and the parish began to develop evangelism training and to produce their own materials. Positive experiences with the various Billy Graham Crusades over the years meant that David and Robyn were not slow to get St Matthew's involved in the 1985 Leighton Ford Sydney Celebration mission.[4]

Prayer for all of the outreach and ministries was also strongly emphasized. Extra prayer meetings were begun, and some Prayer Days were held at Wentworth Falls.

Numbers were growing, especially in the youth work, with an increase in young people taking active leadership roles. The evening service, which had had a congregation of about 30 or so, built up quickly in a year, and was soon packed out. The style of music was updated, and drama started to be used as a teaching tool. The church had moved on from being an 'old fashioned' traditional kind of parish.[5] The growth in numbers led to a financial growth and the need for building extensions!

---

[4] This step would have huge consequences for Robyn's ministry in later years.
[5] According to Alan Hohne 2005

Growth in numbers is always exciting for a church, and David, who freely admits to being a 'big crowds' sort of person, was enjoying it. But more important to any fellowship of Christians is growth in the depth of the spiritual life.

Part of this came about by following Dudley Foord's example of involving everyone in ministry. David began to teach and talk about ministry gifts, encouraging people to use their gifts for the good of the congregation.

In services, he would invite people to be interviewed about their experiences. If a congregation member was going overseas on a business trip, he encouraged them to put on a breakfast for their business contacts and share about their faith, and would pray for them in church.

To emphasise the point weekly, the church bulletin contact list read: 'Ministry team - all the congregation', followed by David's name and phone number.

The idea was being taken up by the congregation. The Wardens Report in 1983 stated firmly, "The body of Christ will only be built up in this place if each believer uses God-given spiritual gifts for the benefit of the congregation as a whole."

And David put this into action. The already existing able team of lay people were encouraged and empowered to lead ministries and to preach while David was away. St Matthew's even took on the challenge of helping out a less well-resourced church with finances and people power when it was looking for a new minister.

"Everything was done and run by the lay people, who were pastored by David," remembers Alan Hohne.[6] "That was the big turning point of West Pennant Hills starting to grow – the working together in those years. It's gone on and on since then."

David wasn't neglecting the traditionally ignored creative gifts of his congregation either. In 1984, some of the young people

[6] Interview with Alan Hohne, 2005

performed a dance, to Christian singer Keith Green's music at a houseparty. From there a St Matthew's dance group grew in size and ability, performing at church and the annual Christian music festival Blackstump.

One parishioner with these gifts greatly appreciated it: "I thank God for the opportunity to experiment and try new things at St Matthew's... it was a great way ... to work in a different form to communicate God's good news," she said.[7]

A more controversial encouragement of ministry gifts was given to women. Robyn and David had long been strong advocates of women's ministry in church, including women's ordination. The mid to late 1980s was a real period of foment in the Sydney Diocese over women's ordination, and David and Robyn came up against a small but vocal core of resistance at meetings and at parish council.[8]

David asked Jill Anstey to be the first female server at communion and the first female Synod representative. She also served for some years on the Parish Council. When he also asked her to preach on a missionary topic, he had to withstand opposition for having a woman speak.

Some of this opposition was quelled by patience and persistence over several years, as well as good experiences with women preachers. One Sunday when David was ill, he had no-one to ask to take over except for Robyn, who gave his sermon with her usual flair and aplomb. It was well received, and she began to speak more and more.

More of the opposition was quelled by special days set aside for discussions, Bible study and prayer about different issues, including one on women's ordination.

---

[7] Phillippa Oakden-Patch in *A history of St Matthew's Anglican Church* by Judy Taylor, 1996.

[8] It was during the 1980s that Robyn was appointed by Synod as the first woman to the Moore Theological College Committee. She continued as the only woman on the committee for a number of years. She recalls some interesting discussions on women in ministry during these meetings.

Jill Anstey wrote later: "David and Robyn were both so forgiving and gracious, and also so patient yet unswerving, that by the time they left us women in ministry were accepted by all but a handful of the congregation."

Even the handful that did not accept it could not fault David's approach to the question. Alan Hohne, long against women's priesting, and one of David's more vocal opponents on parish council, still believes that, whatever David's views were on any question, he always got there by thinking theologically, not just pragmatically. The women issue was discussed prayerfully and in depth on many occasions, and he was always impressed by David's godly approach, even if he didn't agree with his conclusions.[9]

The day discussions were just one part of the teaching program at St Matthew's. Regular weekly sermons were planned three or four months in advance, and linked to the Bible studies for the parish fellowship groups. The sermons were usually short and well-delivered, even with the occasional distraction such as Kim's cat walking into church and down the aisle!

David was reasonably unflappable if things went wrong in services. In a wedding he was conducting, the best man fainted in the middle of the ceremony. He was neatly caught by the bride's father and laid out on the chairs in front of the pews, without a pause or hesitation by David, who was in the middle of reading the ceremony.[10]

Pastoral care of their congregation was one of David's and Robyn's priorities. This came out of the example of Robyn's parents, but also David's own painful childhood and what he saw of the needs of the young people involved in the Jesus Movement. The Claydons made it their particular ministry to be available to people, and the church felt pastored by them.[11]

[9] Interview with Alan Hohne, 2005.
[10] David and Robin More's recollection in *A history of St Matthew's Anglican Church* by Judy Taylor, 1996.
[11] According to Alan Hohne.

Their approach was to address and solve the problems where possible, rather than just to cope with them. Geoff Bartlett, the Rector's Warden, came down with a serious bout of depression, but for no discernible reason. Nothing in his life seemed to have brought it on, but he was struggling badly. David began to meet with him regularly each week, to go for a long walk and a talk with him. The depression still wasn't getting any better, so, one day when his wife Dearnne popped in, David prayed with her: "Lord, show us the answer to this problem."

The answer came very quickly. David suddenly remembered he had been visiting someone else who had been depressed because of a food allergy. "Has Geoff had a change to his diet recently?" he asked Dearnne. In fact, Geoff had gone overboard on a health kick and was eating wheat germ, which was in turn affecting his mood. Once he reduced this, he went back to normal, and the problem was solved.[12]

While David mentored some of the young men, many of the women would talk to Robyn and seek out her friendship and advice. She and David made it a point to do hospital and home visiting together. She would go into school late, or come home early, or even at lunch time to visit people. A difficult time in the parish came when one lady was diagnosed with, and subsequently died from, leukaemia. Her friend, Jill Anstey, remembers David and Robyn being there for her pastorally and by helping out in practical ways.

Parishioners were always welcome at the Rectory, although Robyn's ministry didn't necessarily extend to entertaining them with overly lavish feasts or gourmet cooking.

One of Robyn's gifts was having the energy to be 'in everything'. She was always at the regular prayer meetings and went to every service, just like she had done growing up in her clergy family. Robyn was fortunate to love parish ministry and to be incredibly enthusiastic about it. She enjoyed spending time with people, and

[12] According to Geoff Bartlett, interview 2005.

would encourage them with stories and advice. The whole parish saw her and David as a 'unit' who talked their decisions through together and supported each other.

David's major regret about his ministry at St Matthew's was that he was not able to effectively create a public identity for the church in the community. He had wanted to see the church be more involved in the structures of the local neighbourhood, and to be seen to be a viable and important part of West Pennant Hills. Christmas times offered the opportunity to stage Carols by Candlelight events, and people packed the church for the Christmas services, but, apart from that, the church's profile was disappointing. This may have been because of the physical layout of West Pennant Hills, its proximity to other, larger places with bigger town centres, and the fact that it had no community township centre.

Even if the church found it hard to create a strong local identity, it was not ignoring the world around it. David was continuing with his South Pacific trips, and many of his SU contacts came to share with the St Matthew's congregation. St Matthew's had always been a church with a firm mission focus, but this became stronger and mission giving increased. The visits were not just confined to Pacific Islanders or locally supported missionaries either. One group of Vietnamese boat people was invited to share their stories of how they had become Christians. It was a moving experience for the congregation.

In all churches there are conflicts, and St Matthew's was not immune to differences of opinion over theological issues or directions in ministry. Despite these, however, one parish councillor, Alan Hohne, believes that the parish council operated the best he had ever seen it in the years that David was at St Matthew's. Part of the reason for this was David's willingness to trust the lay leaders and to empower people to work together to make decisions. Despite being unafraid to confront people when it was called for, David never presumed to make decisions for the parish council[13], instead seeing them as partners.

David and Robyn enjoyed their parish ministry so much that, when David was first approached about another job, six years into St Matthew's, he said "No" without even thinking seriously about it.

But God had some other ideas, and, in 1987, David and Robyn found themselves having to say goodbye to the congregation and move on. In the meantime Kim's wedding to David Barker had taken place in April. The Parish had been very excited about the wedding, and a parishioner, Win Leembruggen, had made Kim's wedding gown.

The announcement that the Claydons would be leaving at the end of the year was a sad time, both for the Claydons and for the church, which had deeply appreciated them personally, their ministry, and their enthusiasm and love for Christ and the church. When in the service David announced they would be leaving, someone yelled out from the pews, "Offer him more money!"

After fond farewells, tears and many messages of love and support, the Claydons moved out of the West Pennant Hills Rectory, and on to the next phase of their life.[14]

Strangely enough, the next job was one that fitted perfectly with David's background and Christian heritage. His main influences from Lora and from the Claydon family were Scripture Union, parish ministry, and of course, the Church Missionary Society.

It had come full circle. David was going to be the Federal Secretary of CMS.

---

[13] According to Alan Hohne 2005.

[14] The Claydons stayed in contact with St Matthew's and even now frequently visit the church and members of the congregations.

CMS GOES FROM NOSTALGIC TO STRATEGIC

While many of the congregation of St Matthew's cried when they heard that David and Robyn were leaving, one person was secretly rubbing his hands with delight.

Alan Hohne, who had worked very hard as a nominator to get David to St Matthew's, had worked equally hard to get him out of St Matthew's – not because he didn't like him, but because he thought he was the right person to head another ministry in which Alan was involved: the Church Missionary Society.

CMS was about 180 years old, with a solid history of evangelical missionary endeavour. It was made up of a group of concerned evangelicals, mostly in the Anglican church, who sent people, not money, literature or programs, for the advancement of God's kingdom in different parts of the world.[1]

Since the 1930s CMS Australia had had particular interest in North Australia and East Africa, especially Tanzania. In fact, its ministry was so important in establishing the Anglican church there, that one of the questions in the Swahili catechism, alongside theological questions like, "Who is God the Father?" was "What is CMS?"

The missionary stories that came out of Tanzania were often amazing. In one Diocese, a CMS missionary was concerned by slave traders walking their human wares past the local town en route to a market, and organised the local believers in the newly established church to do something about it. They hauled their church bell up

---

[1] CMS' five principles have remained the same since the Society was formed: 1. Follow God's leading. 2. Put money in second place, not first. 3. Begin in a small way. 4. Under God, all depends on the people sent forth. 5. Look for success only from the Spirit of God.

to the top of a hill overlooking the slave route, and kept people on watch duty to ring the bell and alert the town when a trader approached. The Christians then raided the slave train and set the slaves free.

Sixty years later, when David visited the Diocese and was introduced as being the CMS Federal Secretary, there was an outburst of praise and expressions of deep thanks by the freed slaves who were still alive. In seeing what Christian love had done for them, they had responded to the gospel message and had been active members of the church ever since.

Despite its vibrant track record in its traditional fields, however, by the end of the 1980s CMS Australia was perceived to be outdated and limited. The world was changing at a great rate and CMS was finding it hard to keep up. Now Christians were beginning to recognise new areas of need, such as the existence of 'unreached people groups', the great challenge presented by the Muslim world, and the growing populations in mega-cities.

People inside CMS recognised this need to move with the times. When the opening for a new Federal Secretary came along, they were looking for someone who could take CMS on a journey from nostalgic to strategic.

The first time David's name came up, he was asked informally by Bishop John Reid if he would be interested. Frankly, he wasn't. Parish ministry was going well, he and Robyn were happy where they were, and he wasn't keen on being the head of an organization that seemed to be a little behind the times.

"No, thanks," he said.

But his refusal wasn't going to be accepted. Also on the selection committee was Alan Kerr from David's Scripture Union days. He believed that the six years in the parish after Scripture Union had made David warmer, more friendly and more approachable. He knew David had all the strategic thinking abilities needed, and he also now thought he had the pastoral abilities to take on the job.[2] Alan Hohne from St Matthew's also believed David was the right person: "his gifts would never be adequately given opportunity for expression in a parish" he said later.[3] Together they drummed up enough support to officially nominate him.

It was the week of Kim's wedding, and again, David was asked to consider a change. Archbishop Don Robinson, the president of CMS, approached David, this time officially: "This is a significant role," he said, "and you are the person to take the job."

Now David had to think seriously about it. But his concerns were still the same. Would CMS actually want to make changes and take on a new vision? Would they work with a strategic, not a pragmatic approach? Would they happily shed the old-fashioned image?

Don Robinson pressed hard, so David agreed to take his concerns to the committee.

"I have about 14 questions for you, and I need some good answers," he said. "I can't see any reason to leave a very happy situation if I'm going to be knocking my head against a wall".

The committee came through. "We've already been thinking and talking about the way ahead," they explained. "The reason we've invited you to do this job is that we know that you've got the vision and the ability to push us to do it, and get us into the twenty-first century."

The answer seemed clear. And Robyn and Kim were encouraging with their support. From Robyn's point of view, even the travelling wasn't going to be a problem. At least he would be home for more nights than he was at Scripture Union.

---

[2] "David now had a new warmth and spiritual glow. Everything had come together for him," Alan Kerr said later. Interview 2005.

[3] Interview with Alan Hohne 2005.

So at the beginning of 1988, David became the Federal Secretary of the Church Missionary Society.

But even though the committee thought he had the ability to do the job, David was on a steep learning curve. To begin with, he was not qualified in the area of missiology. This was a relatively new discipline which had developed over the previous decades, thinking through the theology of mission and its practical challenges. But there were very few acclaimed missiological thinkers in Australia, and there was almost nowhere to study it in depth except overseas.

David's evenings, although they were spent at home with Robyn, quickly became consumed with reading journals and articles, and he soon took on a formal program of study to bring himself up to speed.

To get official qualifications, he found a Doctor of Ministry course through the Northern Baptist Seminary, Chicago, which seemed to be both theoretical and practical. It allowed David to plan CMS's new strategies as part of the course work, and gave both him and CMS a foundation for moving forward.[4]

David clearly saw himself as a learner in these early years. In his prayer letters to supporters, he wrote: "Missionaries have taught me..."; "Parishioners have taught me..."; "I've learned from conferences..."; "It's good for me to learn..."

His serious attitude to learning wasn't for everyone. Some years later, when Jane Chetty began as his new secretary, she was having some trouble getting all the missionaries' names and locations right.

"You should take the CMS prayer diary home and read it on the train" was David's advice. He certainly would have done that, but Jane just thought it was funny.

---

[4] David's capacity to cope with a very heavy travel program brought him in touch with world church leaders and other missionary leaders and missiologists. Because of the study and travel he became probably Australia's leading missiologist, according to former Victorian General Secretary Bill Graham, 2005.

All of the study and thinking was setting the scene for CMS's new *Vision for the 90s*. This short statement would tell people where CMS was going, and hopefully get them on board to support it. The Vision was the product of input and prayer from lots of people, but David, as the 'chief missiologist'[5] of CMS, became the driving force, leading the committees through the process.[6]

Essentially it focused on identifying key unreached people groups that CMS could reach out to. Whereas before, missionaries were sent to specific geographic areas, now they would be sent to ministries outlined in the Vision, even if it was in an area that CMS.[7]

One of these new areas was Europe. One of the particular ministries identified by the Vision was university student outreach.[8] When Owen and Catherine Chadwick applied to be CMS missionaries working amongst students, they had in mind a location which would have seemed outrageous to CMS in previous years. They wanted to go to France.

Their reasons were good: France, like much of Europe, was a post-Christian country. Students came from all over North Africa and Europe to study in Paris. The need for evangelism was great, and the Chadwicks had been praying about it.

It was a big step for CMS, but it fit the Vision and they took it on. David spent many hours explaining and justifying the decision to doubting supporters over the next few years.

---

[5] According to former General Secretary of NSW Branch, John Menear, interview 2005. He said: "The Federal Secretary is the person who gives the lead in thinking about directions in missionary trends and directions. David did an excellent job of that."

[6] According to Bill Graham 2005.

[7] In fact, the number of new countries that CMS missionaries were working in grew rapidly (in David's years from 15 to 24) because of the Vision.

[8] Getting into student ministry was not all CMS's idea. There had been a movement swelling and growing in Sydney towards international student work for several years, with groups of people praying towards new opportunities. CMS got on board in the nick of time, according to Alan Hohne, 2005.

But the more the Vision was explained[9] in churches, the more support it seemed to get. CMS was successful, both in broadening its support base amongst younger people and in sending out more missionaries. Without alienating its older support base, and without abandoning its principles, its gospel focus and its sense of history, it was successfully making the transition from folksy, old-fashioned and nostalgic to relevant, strategic and new.

Getting a Vision in place and working took time, persuasion and patience. CMS's strength has always been its grass-roots support base and the way ordinary members can have a say through committees. Unfortunately, its weakness comes from the same source: the committees are often unwieldy and getting things done takes time!

And there are always going to be tensions. David, while selected for his ability to move CMS into the future, also faced some suspicions from some committee members. Firstly, although he had grown up in another culture as a child and had worked with SU in the Pacific area, he had never been a 'proper' missionary himself. How would he be able to relate to the missionaries on the field? Secondly, although he had a good knowledge of CMS, he was really a newcomer. Where would he lead the Society? Finally, although he was a committed evangelical and focused on biblical truths, he had shown himself to be an independent thinker on matters such as the ordination of women. This would set him up for a few clashes over time.

David spent much of his time in committee meetings[10], amongst

[9] The original Vision for the 90s was: to work with national churches especially in training local people; and to expand evangelism and ministry among urban dwellers and students and to make positive contact with Muslims. The Statement was tweaked and reframed slightly in the following decade.

[10] According to former CMS Chairman Peter Chiswell in 2005, David usually took notes on his computer during meetings. Occasionally he would multi-task and unobtrusively do something else like practise learning Chinese while the meeting was going on around him. However, Peter never saw him lose the thread of the discussion.

not a few strong personalities.[11] While some debates were spirited, David never lost his temper[12], although he did occasionally lose an argument. This was sometimes because members of the committee knew more about his chosen topic than he did.[13] Colin Reed characterised his leading of meetings (which sometimes had the potential to be inflammatory) as 'patient and tolerant'.[14] Former CMS President, Archbishop Harry Goodhew, was impressed by David's ability to convey needs and opportunities to the committees through clear, well presented material.[15]

Just as in previous years, his usual tactic was to talk, persuade and convince, before actually introducing the issue. One year, after attending a missions conference in the Middle East, David came back very excited about placing missionaries in the former USSR. The opportunities were there, and it seemed to fit with the Vision. He spent the next two years talking about it, investigating and explaining it until it got the committee support it needed.

Another large administrative and pastoral task was to help the different State Branches of CMS keep working well together. Each Branch is different in size, in history and in situation. The smaller Branches support only a handful of missionaries, and operate as a

---

[11] According to Peter Chiswell, strong personalities can lead to a creative committee!

[12] According to Mary Lewis, who sat on many of the committees over the years. Alan Hohne, who had different ideas to David on student ministry agrees. "Whatever the difference or subject, he never got personal and he never got irrational, and he never badmouthed his opponents. He was always able to maintain warmth in the relationship and his emotions were under control because of his self-discipline." Even John Menear, who openly admitted in 2005 to having had a 'tempestuous' relationship with David, said, "You could get in his face in an argument, but rarely see anger or temper. He absorbed a lot of aggravation, but would come and resolve issues. I think he would have thought that most problems could be solved just by working through the issues."

[13] Bill Graham once caught him out making a sweeping statement about Latin American culture, which Bill, a former missionary in Latin America, disagreed with. "Because he had a sharp analytical mind that quickly got to the heart of issues, he sometimes professed to be an authority on things about which he was not," was Bill's comment in 2005. But he added, "David was essentially a humble person."

[14] Letter from Colin Reed, former principal of St Andrew's Hall, the CMS Training College, 2002.

[15] Interview with Harry Goodhew 2005.

minority evangelical voice in non-evangelical dioceses. The largest Branch, New South Wales, supports the majority of missionaries, raises the most funds and is a well-accepted organization in a strongly 'word-oriented' evangelical environment. The other difficulty was that while the Branches raise the funds, the Federal office spends the money! David worked hard at achieving a balanced federalism, and considering the needs of all the Branches, no matter what the size.[16]

David's thinking, writing, leadership in meetings and administration were just what the nominations committee had been looking for. The thing they perhaps hadn't factored in, but which they came quickly to appreciate, was his work capacity.

He had never lost his ability to put every minute to good use, and with the size of his job and the amount of overseas travel involved, he needed it more than ever. The hours on plane flights were still used to read and dictate reports, to plan meetings and to write letters. He even managed to write a book on cross-cultural evangelism in the time he spent in airport lounges.[17]

The amount of work generated overseas and on the plane meant a big increase for office staff when David arrived back in Sydney. Taking a collective deep breath they would tackle the piles of paperwork and attend to the numerous little notes left on desks. Life was less busy while he was away!

Alan Hohne believes that David was almost too productive. "We got ourselves into assuming that all that work can be done!" he said later.[18] "I think the combination of David's work capacity and skills saved CMS from extinction."

---

[16] According to the CMS Minute of Appreciation on David's retirement in 2002.
[17] *Only Connect* sold 3,000 copies in Australia. It was republished in 2001 as *Connecting Across Cultures*.
[18] Interview with Alan Hohne 2005.

But while CMS was not ready to become extinct quite yet, dedicated readers of these chapters may have a burning question which has not been answered: Wasn't David supposed to be dead by now?

Back in his twenties, a cardiologist had given David only ten years or so to live. Clearly, however, he was still very much alive and kicking. And he was taking on more and more stressful tasks. How had this happened?

At age 31, while staying with a doctor friend, he had mentioned his continuing chest pains again.

"It's not where you normally get heart pains, but you should see someone," said his friend. So this time David went to the head of thoracic medicine at Sydney's Royal Prince Alfred Hospital.

The diagnosis was slightly more specific. "You've got a valve problem and you need annual checkups," he said.

So every year, David had his heart checked. In 1992, with another change of doctor, he had an even more up-to-date diagnosis. And three years later, in 1995, he was told that the time had finally come. He would have to undergo open heart surgery.

This was a shock. Heart surgery was far newer and much more risky than it is now. And the complications could have been fatal. For the first time David was upset about it, and, for the first time in his life, he was angry with God.

"Well, God, you've given me such a tough childhood, and now I've got to have surgery, and the risks of stroke or dying are huge," he complained.

Thankfully the moment questioning was short-lived, and David repented of his outburst and apologized to his heavenly father the very next day.

And God was very gracious and faithful to him. The surgery went fine. Even the three months he had to take off work were well-used! True to form, in the weeks before and after the operation he used the computer at home[19], answered all his emails, planned some papers and put together two CMS magazines. A few weeks of annual holidays finished off his recovery period and he was ready to get back to work.

---

[19] David was appreciative of John Menear's computer skills and the way he set up a computer and email facility for him at home, enabling David to keep up with the work.

CHAPTER TWENTY ONE

MAN OF THE WORLD

David's first trip to Africa nearly saw him end up in a jail cell. He had decided to make his first overseas trip visiting CMS missionaries in Tanzania, Kenya and Zaire[1]. Things were working out to get to the first two countries, but obtaining a visa to enter Zaire was more easily said than done.

"What you'll have to do is to get a MAF[2] flight from Tanzania across to Zaire and land at the airport in Bukavu," advised David's colleague, Ross Hall, who had plenty of African experience. "You'll officially be 'in transit' so you won't need the visa. Get our missionary to come and chat to you there."

David took his advice, and landed in the small plane at the rudimentary Bukavu 'airport', consisting of an airstrip and a tin shed. CMS's Margaret Lawry[3] explained to the soldier on duty that she needed to talk to David, and came out to the plane to chat. But the sun was beating down and David was rapidly getting hotter, so he got out, intending to stand under the wing of the plane.

The minute he reached the door of the plane, the soldier on duty came over to arrest him for having no visa, and took his passport.

Margaret Lawry tried her best to get David off the hook, but the guard was not giving any ground. He may have been expecting a pay-off, but CMS has a 'no-bribe' policy, and David was not going to pay for his freedom. When Margaret eventually had to go after an hour or so, David took over, and, in bad French, kept trying to explain the

---

[1] Now the Democratic Republic of Congo.

[2] Missionary Aviation Fellowship run a vital network of small aeroplanes in remote parts of the world, transporting and servicing Christian workers. MAF planes are usually small, light aircraft.

[3] Whom Robyn had taught as a pupil at Queenwood.

same things over and over: "I'm just here on the plane. I'm not entering the country!"

By this time David and the guard were standing in the tin shed and the MAF pilot was getting impatient. The plane needed to leave! So the pilot took his turn at trying to negotiate his passenger's freedom. David was hot and dehydrating so he went to the door of the shed to get some air. And he began to pray.

"Lord, all those folk back home are praying for me – for their sake, please resolve this situation."

At that moment, an immaculately-dressed African man, carrying a large pile of letters, walked across the airstrip and tucked his letters under the front seat of the MAF plane.

"He must have something to do with MAF," David thought, and called out in his basic French, "Can you help me?"

The man came over, and, in perfect English, said, "How can I help you?"

David explained the dilemma, so the man went in to talk to the guard. In about five minutes, he came back to David with a smile on his face.

"It's fine," he said. "You'll just have to apologise to him. I know you haven't done anything wrong, but he's lost face, so if you apologise he'll give you your passport back and you can go."

David rushed across to apologise, and then turned back to thank his benefactor, but he had gone. He looked out of the door, but the man had disappeared completely. The large airport area was flat and clear, and there was nowhere he could have gone in such a short time without being seen.

The pilot was keen to get going, so he hurried David onto the plane. Once they took off, David tried to find out what had happened.

David asked the pilot, "Who was that man who helped me and brought some mail? Is he a MAF representative?"

"I don't know. We don't have anyone like that here," said the pilot, also at a loss. David said, "Have a look at what he brought!"

But under the seat was nothing - no letters at all!

It seemed to David that he had been supernaturally rescued[4], but just to satisfy his curiosity, he wrote to Margaret Lawry. To be so well-dressed and to speak perfect English in Zaire is very rare, and he knew that Margaret would know him if he was local.

"There's no such person that I know of," she wrote back. And so David praised God for his rescue!

The story was a real encouragement for David's and Robyn's prayer supporters.[5] When David was appointed to CMS, he asked all the churches he had been linked with to pray for him and Robyn. They maintained the connection with regular letters, telling about their travels and their upcoming movements, and David would often bump into someone who could tell him what he was about to do or had been doing that day, because he had been praying for him.

The prayer support was a real source of strength for David. And he needed it. A large and tiring part of his job as Federal Secretary was to travel around the world[6], visiting missionaries, looking at opportunities for future ministry, and talking with church leaders about the needs of their area.

The issues in each location were many and varied. In one trip, David would have to sort through a plethora of information on all sorts of different topics.

On his first visit to East Africa, he looked at the local Bible colleges in Kenya, the possibility for development ministries in arid

---

[4] David often wonders what exactly the man said to the soldier to persuade him to give David his freedom so quickly, after at least an hour of tough negotiating. He had been watching the whole conversation closely, and saw no money change hands, so there were no bribes involved!

[5] The prayer supporters were members of St Matthew's West Pennant Hills, St Alban's Lindfield, Christ Church St Ives, St Swithun's Pymble and St Philip's South Turramurra where David and Robyn had become members when David took up his CMS role.

[6] David spent at least four months of the year overseas and in North Australia, visiting about 20 countries.

regions, the changing population dynamics from rural to urban all over Kenya, and a missionary school that needed staff.

Tanzania's issues on the same trip included dealing with work permits and immigration difficulties for missionaries, the need for secretarial staff in some Dioceses, and the fact that, when goods were shipped from Australia to Tanzania, soap should not be wrapped with food because the soapy taste comes through!

As well as sorting through needs and opportunities, he also had to come to grips with the realities of the ministries that missionaries were engaged with. While visiting Alf and Nola Chipman in Kenya, news came that the local Masai witch doctor had become a Christian through listening to tapes which Alf had produced and circulated. Alf was thrilled and set off with David to find the man.

David had never had an experience like this, and was unsure as to whether a witch doctor could really let Jesus be Lord of his life, so he chatted to him and asked, "What does this mean for your work as a Masai witch doctor?"

"Oh," he said, "I sold my practice to my brother."

He then sent his family out to gather together all the other Masai people whom he had led to the Lord, and proceeded to preach an excellent sermon on a text from Luke's gospel!

The realities of the needs of so many people and Christian fellowships in so many parts of the world could be fairly stark. On another trip to Africa, a pastor walked 80km to have lunch with David, and asked for a CMS missionary for his area.

In Japan, speaking at a student rally, David talked to three students who told him how much they were challenged by his message. David was about to be pleased, but then they said, "However, we will not be able to be Christians for another 25 years."

At first he thought there was something wrong in the translation. But they explained that in Japanese companies, people have to engage in Shintoistic rituals if they want to be promoted.

The students had all just found jobs in the same firm, and knew that in 25 years time they would be sufficiently senior to be able to say no to participating in the rituals. In the meantime they would just have to take part if they wanted to keep advancing.

This was illustrated the next day, at church, when David met a Christian man who had refused to be involved in the rituals, and, as a result, had not been promoted beyond first year level. In Japan, when people introduce themselves, they start by stating their company and their level. Children at school have to give their father's company and status when they introduce themselves to a new teacher or class. This man had two daughters who were embarrassed because their father's income was so low and his status so minimal. His faithfulness to Christ was costly.

A similar story emerged when David had the opportunity to talk about Christ to teenagers living in an African slum. Their response? "Yes, we know about Jesus, but if we follow him, we can't steal. We can't get work in this slum and we can't live anywhere else. There's no other way to survive except by stealing!"

The big challenge was to sort through all the information and present it to CMS back in Australia for their prayers and decisions.

But David was not just limited to seeing what the Australian church could do through CMS. He also had a larger view – to empower other national churches and to work with other organisations to best take up the opportunities. It was here that his love for networking came into play.

When Alec Baker lost his job in management consulting in Australia, he thought perhaps God had something for him overseas. He rang David to find out if there was something he could offer to CMS.

"Hallelujah" was David's initial reaction to Alec's news. He then networked to set the Bakers up to share their expertise with a Christian media organisation in the Middle East.

David networked for EFAC[7] also, as the Australasian representative on its International Executive Committee, and was able to help some bishops in the third world set up structures to allow their churches to be missionary-sending churches, as well as missionary-receiving churches.

Bill Graham believes that, because David was comfortable with many different kinds of people, including those who did not share his point of view, he was able to make a very broad range of contacts across the world. As a person of substance himself, he was not overawed by the 'top people' in organisations, and was respected as someone who knew what he was talking about.[8]

Alan Hohne recalls that CMS had very good relationships with quite wide networks because of David. "We progressed wonderfully because of those relationships", he said later.[9] In fact, the placement of most of the missionaries doing student ministry in Europe came out of David's ability to build relationships.[10]

The networking relationships often became personal friendships. David later wrote, "I've developed an enormous circle of friends in many countries, and my email in-basket is dominated by their prayer or newsletters."[11]

Bishop Mouneer from Egypt was one particular friend who felt 'able to share his heart frankly'. "During the years I have found that he related to me ... on the level of a personal friend and not just as a partner in mission," he said.[12]

The good relationship with Mouneer may have been strengthened because of David's natural love for Egypt, based on

---

[7] The Evangelical Fellowship of the Anglican Communion.

[8] According to John Menear, 2005.

[9] Alan Hohne's only criticism was that often they were David's relationships rather than CMS's relationships. "Later we found we didn't know people at the level we really needed," he said in 2005.

[10] According to John Menear, 2005.

[11] Writing in Checkpoint as he left CMS in 2002.

[12] Letter in 2002.

happy childhood memories. Because of this, and because of David's particular interest in ministry to Muslims, the bishop made him an honorary Canon of Cairo's All Saints' Cathedral. Egypt, and also Singapore, because of his many old friends there from university days, were probably his two favourite places to visit.

But another favourite place, even despite his dislike of the curried lentils served up at nearly every meal, was Nepal. This tiny Hindu Kingdom has only been open to Christian mission since 1954. Most of the mission organisations, including CMS, still work together under the umbrella of the United Mission to Nepal, which was the largest non-government employer in Nepal in 1991, with 2,500 Nepali and more than 300 expatriate workers.

The UMN board met once a year for five days to decide policy and direction for this sprawling organisation. With 60 representatives from different mission boards of different denominations of more than 20 countries, the meetings had potential for both greatness and strife! David was the chairman for six years, and engaged in 'pure relationship building and negotiation', according to UMN missionary Mary Lewis.

David seemed to have a soft spot for the Nepali church[13], and he worked hard both to guide UMN in strategic ministries and to build up the young Nepali church, especially through helping to set up effective theological education.

South America was another area where networking and building good structures meant a useful growth in mission. Both CMS and another Anglican agency, SAMS,[14] had been working in South America. During David's visits to missionaries and bishops in Latin America he was asked to think about consolidating the missionary work under one organization. Senior Australian Bishops were also keen to see the two brought together. The arrangements, with all

[13] According to Nepal's Dr Ramesh Khatry, 2002
[14] South American Missionary Society

the potential for division and hurt, were pursued successfully.[15]

The exciting work of seeing national churches grow and ministries begin may have been the 'glamorous' side of the job, but the hassles of travel and exposure to the more grungy aspects of life were still a part of it.

Some things were just plain revolting. In one country, Robyn and David were eating in a 'tea house'. David needed to use the facilities and was led to a place under the building. Outside he saw chickens eating the scraps straight off the dirty plates from the tea house upstairs. Thinking this was probably a good way to use up the scraps, he wasn't too concerned, until he saw the actual method of washing up – letting the dogs lick the plates clean! When he sat down again at the table he said nothing about it, but ate nothing that had touched the plate.

Other things were just plain dangerous. In Nepal, David was visiting missionaries Tim and Joy Linton. Their house was small, so they arranged for him to sleep in another house on the hospital campus which had a spare bed. As they walked down together, Tim pointed to a spot on the track where the previous evening there had been a leopard.

David knew he had to walk up again later for dinner, so he asked the obvious question: "What if there is a leopard on the track?"

"No worries", said Tim, "they only eat children and chickens." When dinner time finally came David walked up to the Linton home praying hard all the way!

Leopards may only have eaten children, but crocodiles eat adults, and, in North Australia, David was told to choose a different route each day for his early morning walk.

[15] The then General Secretary of SAMS, Revd Brian Viney, took the initiative to pursue this matter with his committee and with David. Once agreement had been reached between SAMS and CMS, David sent Bill and Barbara Graham (the then Victorian CMS General Secretary and previously missionaries in Peru) to meet with all the SAMS and CMS missionaries, and the bishops in Latin America, to discuss the new arrangement and to assure SAMS missionaries that they would be fully supported by CMS, and that their arrangements under SAMS would be maintained.

"The crocodiles watch you, and, after three days, they work out your patterns and then pounce on you," he was told. He didn't try to disprove the statement.

Inevitably, however, David would arrive home in Australia, ready to talk about where he had been, and present information, stories and ideas. His principles for jet-lag free travel (no red meat, alcohol, tea or coffee, don't eat a meal in the middle of the night and keep moving around) usually meant he could walk straight back into the office, but on rare occasions after a trip his secretary would go into his office to find him asleep at his desk.[16] She would back out quietly, his secret safe with her.

It could have been easy for David, having gained such a broad picture of what God was doing in the world, to feel angry or impatient with Australian churches and Christians who just 'didn't get it'. But he took the view that part of his role was to teach and challenge the church back home. Usually presenting the bigger picture excited people and resulted in not only a new understanding, but a good response of commitment.

He seemed to have a special gift of being able to master, popularise and communicate vast amounts of information and make it accessible to those who did not have the opportunity or the background to do the same.[17] His particular style of talk was to give a comprehensive overview of Christian missions and relate it to current historical, political and social issues.[18]

Many of these issues seemed depressing: committed Christians in the minority, stories of persecuted churches, complete economic breakdown in countries like Zaire, and the huge needs for Christian

---

[16] According to Jane Chetty, 2005.

[17] According to Bill Graham, 2005.

[18] Janine Stewart of CMS Victoria believes that David's great contribution to CMS was his broad and deep understanding of mission around the world, and the issues facing the churches. His 'world view' sessions at the Victorian annual conference were always much looked forward to, much talked about, and much appreciated. Letter 2005.

workers in almost every area of the world. In the mid-nineties, before Islamic militancy came into the popular news, David was talking about its future effect on churches and ministry strategies.[19]

But even if the news was miserable, David did not let his talks end on a defeated note. He always emphasised God's victory, rooting his optimism firmly in the Scriptures. From there he could encourage his audience to reach out and to support mission work in the wider world.[20]

David was not only interested in encouraging traditionally strong evangelical churches to support mission, but he was also very willing to visit and speak in areas where the Anglican church had a different flavour. Although David's theological views were strongly conservative evangelical[21], he had the ability to be 'Sydney-based, but not Sydney-centric'[22], with an openness to people who held different points of view. He frequently spoke at conferences that combined people of widely differing viewpoints[23], and built many bridges for CMS.

But whether his audiences were made up of traditional CMS supporters, local parish churches, or clergy, they seemed to appreciate his input. In 1998, a sermon and seminar at St Columb's Anglican Church in Hawthorn, Victoria, "were used by God spiritually in people's lives... It will enhance our support for CMS's gospel ministries."[24]

Thankfully it was only very occasionally that he would get a small-minded response like the comment from one church: "Well, CMS should send *us* a missionary to do outreach in *our* parish!"

---

[19] In fact, David's particular interest during his time at CMS and since, has been Islam, and he is often invited to give Christian groups a background to the current news stories.

20 John Reid said, in 2005, that David tended to soak up other people's views and give them as his own views. His comment was: "This, at its best, was impressive; on the other hand, you marvelled that one person could speak so authoritatively on so many parts of the world."

But the fact was that David *did* travel widely. He visited many more places than the 25 or so countries where CMS missionaries were working, and he spoke to many more people than he 'had' to for his job. The stories he used were almost always first hand, or from very reliable sources. Stories and contacts from Robyn's travels added to these, and he had always worked hard at staying informed and reading widely.

21 John Reid said in 2005, "He was always a gospel man."

22 According to Andrew Lake, 2002.

23 For example, he was on the General Synod's Mission and Ecumenical Commission for a time and was also used as a Consultant in the Melbourne 'Theology of Mission' commission.

24 Letter from Neil Bach at St Columb's Hawthorn, Victoria, 1998.

CHAPTER TWENTY TWO

USE THE WOMEN'S GIFTS TOO!

The year was 1991. The Iron Curtain had fallen in the Soviet bloc just two weeks earlier. And Robyn Claydon was in Russia, about to speak to the congregation of the Moscow Baptist Church.

As she walked up the steps to the platform accompanied by eleven men in dark suits and Vera Kadaeva, her translator, Vera whispered in her ear, "They've asked you to give a message from the Bible. That's wonderful: we don't usually have women giving the message."

On the platform, Robyn waited to hear the only word she recognised – her name - and then got up to speak on the first chapter of Philippians. The room was an amazing sight. Every seat and every square foot of room was packed with people rugged up against the bitter Moscow cold.

She told the church how their brothers and sisters around the world had been praying for them, and spoke on Paul's words: "I thank God every time I remember you. In all my prayers for you, I pray with joy".[1]

It was a long way from Sydney to Moscow, and Robyn had taken a long journey to get there.

Teaching at Abbotsleigh School had been Robyn's joy and privilege for years.

"I loved it and I never thought that I would give it up. It was in my blood," she said later. She particularly loved the opportunities for Christian witness, but, in 1982, a chain of events began that would give her a much wider scope for that witness.

Leighton Ford was an evangelist with Billy Graham's organisation, and was in Sydney for an outreach campaign. Robyn

---

[1] Story quoted in *Looking Forward to the Rest of your life?* Lorry Lutz 2004 Baker Books Grand Rapids, MI.

had helped with puppet and drama presentations for the evangelistic programs, and she invited him to speak at Abbotsleigh to students and staff during his time in Sydney. She may have been a little carried away by the moment when she said to him, "If you ever need a woman to speak in women's meetings in your crusades, I'd love to do it."

Nothing came of it for a couple of years, but, in 1985, she got a phone call asking her to serve on the planning committee of the Lausanne II Conference, to be held in Manila in 1989. Officially she represented the Oceania region, and, as the only, and possibly the 'token' woman on the small, ten-member committee, she became a member of the planning committee and the leader of the 'Women's Track'.

It was a conference which would change her life. From childhood, Robyn had always loved to tell others about Jesus. And as she had been encouraged herself, she had always loved to encourage women to use their God-given gifts. Lausanne II brought both of these two passions into focus and gave her a new task.

The Lausanne conference in 1974 had included only a few hundred women delegates, one female workshop presenter, and no women plenary speakers. But, for Lausanne II, the committee decided to invite women to be fully involved in leading the congress, presenting plenary papers, chairing full congress sessions, speaking at workshops and preaching at the communion service.

And each country was asked to make sure that at least a quarter of people attending from their nation were women.

"If we can't find enough women to fill up the 25 per cent, can we send more men?" came the question from some country groups.

But the answer was "No. The gifted Christian women are there. Look for them."[2]

---

[2] Article: *Women Affirmed in Manila* by Robyn Claydon. South Pacific Journal of Mission Studies. Sept 1990.

A week into the conference, a group of 70 delegates from Russia was enthusiastically welcomed. They had been allowed out by their restrictive communist government to attend. But while Robyn was rejoicing with everyone else at this breakthrough, inwardly she pined, "Where are the Russian Christian women amongst these 70 men?"

In fact, sadly, fewer women turned up to Lausanne II than they had hoped for. Some countries just had not been able to locate enough capable women. But still 900 Christian women from over 150 countries were part of 4,500 delegates who came together to think, pray, share and strategize around the conference slogan - the 'whole church taking the whole gospel to the whole world'.

Robyn could see a problem. The 'whole church' included women - women who were clearly gifted by God, and accountable to him to use their gifts for the spread of the gospel.

The fact that not enough women were found to attend the conference underlined for her that women's ministries were not recognised throughout the world as fully as they should be.

"What is the role of women in world evangelization?" she wrote before the conference. "It is the same as the role of men, that is, to carry out the Great Commission to go into all the world and preach the gospel."[3]

The Women's Track workshops aimed to identify and encourage women at the conference in their task of world evangelization. But part of that was also identifying the things that blocked them.

These 'roadblocks' included a need for clear teaching and Biblical depth for women, so that they could become theologically sound enough to take on leadership roles. There was also a challenge to women to see themselves as accountable to God for their own ministries, and to move out and discover what God had "called,

---

[3] Article *Women and World Evangelization* by Robyn Claydon. 'World Evangelization' the magazine of the Lausanne Committee, Sept/Oct 1987

liberated and equipped them to go out and be".[4]

The obvious roadblock was a basic lack of recognition in some male-dominated cultures where women are expected to be subservient. Before the conference, in a planning meeting in 1987, a Pakistani Bishop had drawn attention to this problem from his own experience:

"Pakistan is a male-dominated society. But I am struggling. My own daughter has the gift of preaching. What can she do?" he lamented.

Iqbal Massey agreed with him: "Thousands of women are burning inside with the message of the gospel, but their lips are sealed because of the culture."

But no matter where they were from, over and over, before and during Lausanne II, women raised the issue of their lack of opportunity to serve. The message that Robyn heard again and again was, "We're not being used; we want to be in team leadership with men; we would like to be allowed to use all our ministry gifts." The overriding consensus from the conference was the desire to see women released to fuller ministry around the world.[5]

Robyn did a good job of planning the Women's Track, but she had also thought through what could be the next step for encouraging women through Lausanne. She proposed that someone should be appointed to co-ordinate and develop the initiatives taken at the Lausanne II conference.

---

[4] According to Evelyn Jensen, adjunct professor at School of World Mission, Fuller Theological Seminary, California. 'Women Urged to Use Ministry Gifts' by Sharon Mumper, in *The Daily News*, the Official Newspaper of Lausanne II in Manila, Issue 4 July 1989.

[5] The 'Manila Manifesto' drawn up at the end of the Conference included 21 Affirmations, one of which said in part, "We affirm that the gifts of the Spirit are distributed to all God's people, women and men, and that their partnership in evangelization must be welcomed for the common good." Other statements in the Manifesto included: "God created men and women as equal bearers of his image, accepts them equally in Christ and poured out his Spirit on all flesh, sons and daughters alike. In addition, because the Holy Spirit distributes his gifts to women as well as to men, they must be given opportunities to exercise their gifts."

She didn't realise that that person would turn out to be her!

With the conference over, David and Robyn returned home to what could have continued to be their normal lives.

But a little while later, Dr Leighton Ford, who at the time was Chair of Lausanne, asked Robyn to become Lausanne's Senior Associate for Women. The job sounded exciting, but huge. If she took it on, she would be networking around the world, speaking, preaching, organising conferences.

And then Dr Ford said, "This would be a voluntary position. You'd need to meet your own expenses."

Robyn first answer was to say 'no'. She had years left in teaching, and she had never planned to leave the job she loved so much. But she just couldn't get the message of the women of Lausanne II out of her mind.

"Use us, encourage us," she kept hearing.

Robyn prayed: "Lord, give me a strong sense of peace if I should move in this direction!"

God answered her prayer with the peace she had asked for, and she continued to think and pray about it with her family. David was travelling overseas a lot with CMS, and Kim was now married and no longer at home, so Robyn was free to travel. Only the money could have been a problem, but David, who had had so much practice at living on prayers as a child, encouraged her to step out in faith.[6]

So, at the end of 1990, Robyn took early retirement from Abbotsleigh and planned her first trip. But the world seemed a big place. Where should she go first, and what would she do?

It was a massive time of change in Eastern Europe. The Iron curtain was falling, so it seemed right to visit the ex-Soviet states. Robyn wrote to a few women from the Czech Republic, Romania,

---

[6] The faith paid off. Robyn paid for her overseas travel out of her own bank account in the first year. As she began telling others about what she was doing, however, people began to ask if they could help. In subsequent years she worked out where she would go and the costs involved and gave the figures to friends. Gifts generally covered all her expenses.

Poland and Russia, but had only a few responses back. When she purchased her ticket to Russia she didn't know if anyone had arranged meetings, or even received her letters.

But as well as having her speak at the Moscow Baptist Church, Vera had arranged other meetings and opportunities for Robyn to encourage women, and she was able to give out Bibles to Scripture-hungry believers and non-believers.

From that small start, Robyn's travels took her into over 50 countries right around the world. Her official title, the Lausanne Senior Associate for Women in World Evangelization, may be a mouthful, but her ministry was practical.

"I do a variety of things, but it's all related to evangelism, either proclaiming the gospel whenever I get an opportunity, or training and building up women so they may be able to do it themselves," she explained in 2000.[7]

And she does get opportunities.

In 2001, she arrived in the US with a friend just after September 11 attacks had occurred. The young woman driving the taxi to their hotel asked why they had come, adding, "It's not a good time to be here."

"We're Christians, and we're coming to a Christian women's conference," said Robyn.

At that the young woman half turned around and said, "Do you know anything about the book of Revelation? Can you explain it to me?"

There were only ten minutes left in their journey, so as they drove, Robyn gave the most speedy explanation of the book of Revelation ever attempted, presenting two pictures, the growth of evil in the world at the hands of Satan, and the wonderful everlasting kingdom that God is preparing for those who love him.

As they arrived at the hotel the young woman said, "I do believe

[7] Interview with Alive Magazine August 2000

that. I am a Christian, but since September 11, I've been so scared. I find myself wondering, if I set off for work one morning having not asked God to forgive my sins of yesterday, and something terrible happened, would God take me to heaven?"

Like so many people, this young woman had some sort of faith, but no assurance. Robyn and her friend, Jill Wallis[8] from Sydney, were able to answer her question and tell her that if she had committed her life to Christ, it was the act of commitment that made her an inheritor of the Kingdom of God, not whether or not she had remembered to pray that morning!

That conversation was Robyn's evangelism for the day, but the rest of the conference, as with the rest of her ministry, was focused on mentoring and encouraging women around the world to do the same, to evangelise and to use their gifts for God.[9]

Robyn had always felt strongly that the list of the spiritual gifts, for example evangelism, teaching, leadership, hospitality and encouragement, which God gives to believers, is not in any way gender-related. As Madelon, her mother, had done for her, her aim was to help women realise that any one or more of these gifts could be given to them, and, in fact, that God had only gifted them so that those gifts can be used!

This came home to Robyn when she met Lee, an American president of a computing consultancy at a pre-Lausanne leadership conference in the US in 1988. In her home church, Lee was only allowed to lead an adult Bible class if there were no men present. At the conference, however, Lee saw women's gifts being freely used to

[8] Jill accompanied Robyn on a number of ministry trips and is an Associate to the Lausanne Women's network. She is also the South Pacific Co-ordinator for Women of Global Action.

[9] The official aims of the Lausanne Women's Network are: 1. Challenging, training, encouraging and mobilizing women for the task of world evangelization. 2. Networking women involved in evangelism and Bible teaching in the world so that ideas can be shared, and prayer support assured. 3. National and regional conferences enabling women leaders to return to their own countries with renewed vision and challenge. 4. Visiting women on location, working alongside them through outreach, teaching, Bible study and spiritual nurture. 5. Mentoring and networking younger women leaders.

build up both women and men, and encountered encouragement for women in ministry and evangelism.

For the first time, she said, clergy treated her, a lay person, as one with them, and men treated her, a woman, as one with them. It was a life-changing experience for Lee to see men and women working together, using their gifts for God.

Lee, a competent, capable and knowledgeable presenter with experience speaking to members of large multinational corporations, spoke at a workshop, and from there was surprised to be invited to speak at a nearby church on the ministry of the laity.

"Here is a dynamic, able Christian woman only just beginning to be used by the church," said Robyn when she told Lee's story later. "How many other Christian women are there waiting for opportunities to use the gifts the Lord has given them?"[10]

Over ten years later, her passion for this subject had not abated. "I find many young women are experiencing a lot of pain. They have gifts and are passionate about using those gifts, but, because of their particular church or denomination, they may not be getting the opportunities they would like to have," she said in an interview in 2000. "I think we've come a long way, but there's still quite a long way to go until the point at which God's gifting of people is what matters, not the gender associated with the gifting."[11]

But even if leaders do have the opportunities to use their gifts, they still need to be found, trained, nurtured, developed and motivated. Robyn's own experience in being mentored by her parents instilled in her a great desire to do the same for others.[12]

[10] "I'd Like a Pulpit for My birthday!" by Robyn Claydon, Jan 1989. Women & World Evangelisation.
[11] Robyn Claydon being interviewed in Alive Magazine August 2000.
[12] According to Robyn, a good mentor: Is prepared to listen; Asks the right questions; Is more interested in the other person than themselves; Is willing to be vulnerable; Trusts and can be trusted; Knows and loves God and has a passion to share the gospel; Knows the scriptures well; Is willing to be helped as much as to help. Looking Forward to the Rest of your life? Lorry Lutz 2004 Baker Books Grand Rapids, MI.

One particular conference Robyn organised in Berlin focused on 20 young women leaders chosen from around the world, and brought together for teaching and encouragement. In other conferences, these young women were given opportunities to use their ministry gifts. On the last day of the Hope for Europe conference[13], 10,000 European women gathered in Frankfurt, and Eva Mrsic, one of the chosen Berlin 20, was given the task to stand up in front of the crowd to speak.

"To experience her encouragement and trust in me in Frankfurt helped me to see the importance of the gift of encouragement," wrote Eva later.[14]

Robyn's love and trust of Eva inspired her to mentor other women in Croatia in the same way. Many of the other 20 women felt privileged to be part of the Berlin conference and were similarly challenged.

"The Berlin group..."turned out to be a real blessing for every one of us," wrote Olga Zaprometova.[15] "The Lord is uniting his church, binding us with his love, overcoming denominational and racial barriers, and giving us one heart full of desire to serve others in joy as we have seen in Robyn!"

The conference helped the women make strong connections of friendship and prayer, which also helped to support their ongoing ministries

Evangeline Sita, an Indian teacher and founder of a Christian high school, still prays for and emails her friends from Berlin. The even wider networks of Lausanne women have helped her in the hard times of sustaining the school.

---

[13] 'Hope for Europe' held in Germany in 1999 encouraged women from over 20 countries. On its last day the 10,000 Christian women from Germany, Austria and Switzerland met together in Frankfurt stadium. It was the first time women from different denominations had ever met together in Germany.

[14] Email from Eva Mrsic 2005

[15] Email from Olga Zaprometova 2005.

Two groups who pray for her hail from Sydney. Robyn's ability to 'introduce' her friends to each other serves both sides well.

"Although I have never seen them, I feel like I know each one of them so well and we uphold one another, pray and support each other," said Evangeline recently.[16]

Many answers to her prayers for her ministry have been remarkable. Evangeline was finding it hard to recruit and keep good Christian teachers at the school. While she was crying out to the Lord each day for answers to her problem, on the other side of the world, another young woman was also crying out to God to show her his will and plan and direct her path.

"I didn't know who she was and she didn't know who I was. But God heard all of our prayers and cries to him and he made a connection," said Evangeline. She received an email from a woman who had been at the Lausanne Forum, asking her if she needed this young woman to teach at her school.

Writing to Robyn after the event Evangeline said, "I did not know what to do but cry and laugh at the same time for the wonderful and great God we have and serve, who hears and answers... Today she's here with me in India. Now wouldn't you call that a wonderful and great act of God's Providence?"

To Robyn's great joy, these young women's gifts are being used.

---

[16] Email from Evangeline Sita, 2005.

Chapter Twenty Three

Faithful where we are

"In the Claydon house, there were David and Robyn, and they always seemed to be going somewhere.[1]"

It was true. David's and Robyn's travel schedules in the 1990s seemed to be equally hectic.[2] Travel had become a major part of their lives and they spent quite a few months of the year apart, meeting up in places like Croatia or Nepal!

"We're trying to provide a model of sharing roles, and we're getting many opportunities to do that. We try to do some things together and some things apart, but we always give time to listening to and affirming each other," said Robyn at the time.[3]

Robyn certainly gained from her husband's travel experiences, and, like him, tried only ever to travel with an overnight bag which she could carry with her on the plane. There's no point in wasting time hanging around an airport luggage carousel.

The pair continued to make a big effort to keep in regular contact with supporters, sending prayer letters and itineraries, and, quite frequently, brief, newsy postcards to particular praying friends. But sometimes they gave more worries than they meant to. One postcard to Geoff and Dearnne Bartlett included this teaser, with no other information: "We nearly got caught in some riots but managed to escape." Perhaps it was intended to inspire more prayer!

Riots were not usually part of Robyn's itinerary, although she met plenty of women who had experienced political troubles.

---

[1] According to Peter Chiswell, Interview 2005.

[2] David's travel itinerary was more constrained by other factors with his job, so Robyn tried to match the timing of her trips to his. They tried to be away at the same time, and in Australia at the same time, and spent much time co-ordinating their diaries.

[3] Interview with Alive Magazine August 2000.

Visiting Eastern Europe in 1991, she met women who had struggled to remain faithful under communism and who were now coming to terms with their newfound political freedom. One woman came 400 km to attend an interdenominational meeting sharing models of evangelism.

"I've never met anyone from another Christian denomination before," the woman said.[4]

Encouraging women was particularly important in the ex-Soviet bloc. In one ex-USSR Islamic state after communism fell, laws outlawing evangelism, public worship and Christian meetings were quickly enacted. One Christian woman leader told Robyn, "It is very hard being a Christian in my country, and it also hard being a woman. We have a saying, 'Chickens are not birds, and women are not people.' Please pray for us![5]"

But for every depressing story, there was an encouraging one as well.

Robyn met Shirinai in 1991 in Moscow. She had been brought up under communism, constantly hearing that there is no God. However, one day, as she walked towards a metro station, she was stopped in her tracks when she heard an elderly Russian man speaking loudly on a street corner.

"I have been imprisoned many times for telling people there is a God," he said. "I might be imprisoned again."

Shirinai was fascinated by both his courage and his message. She stayed to listen and then invited him home to tell her more. The old man stayed for eight hours, telling her there was a God who knew all about her, loved her and wanted her to follow him.

The next day Shirinai took a leaf out of the man's book. She went to a street corner and started to tell these things to the people

---

[4] Interview transcript between Robyn Claydon and John Reid, 1991
[5] Interview transcript between Robyn Claydon and John Reid, 1991

passing by. People stopped to listen, and some asked questions about what she was saying. Shirinai wasn't quite equipped to answer them yet.

"Don't ask me any questions!" she said. "I don't know! All I know is what I heard yesterday, and I'm telling you today!"

When she discovered that there was a God and she could become his child forever by responding to Jesus Christ, there was no way she was going to keep this wonderful news to herself! Now Shirinai is a church planter and can often be found on a Moscow street corner telling people about Jesus.

Another person Robyn met was Sharipa, who grew up in a Central Asian republic in a Muslim family. She had tried to read the Qur'an but she couldn't understand it. Her journey to Jesus began when a friend from a neighbouring country invited her for a week's visit, took her to church and gave her an easy-to-read children's Bible in Russian.

Sharipa enjoyed the stories of Jesus, but thought that, as she was a Muslim, she probably should be reading the Qur'an. She tried again, but she still couldn't understand it.

One night Sharipa had a very vivid dream. She was trying to wash her dirty legs with dirty water, but just couldn't get the grime off. Then she saw a man in shining white, standing near by a river and holding a towel. He beckoned her to come, and washed her legs for her in beautiful clean water.

Sharipa felt sure the man in her dream was the Jesus she had read about in the Bible, and the next Sunday went looking for a Christian church. She told a believer at the church all about her dream.

"It is Jesus," said her new friend. "If you come to him and believe in him, he will wash away your sins."

Sharipa did this, and continued as a strong Christian believer with a great involvement in the small Christian fellowship in her local village.

Robyn's travels took her from Europe to Asia to the Pacific Islands, from Africa to the Middle East, to the US and to the Indian sub-continent. She spoke at conferences, organised meetings, and met with women to teach, encourage and pray. Not all the women she met were what she expected.

In a small Nepali church service, sitting on the floor, Robyn noticed a woman who kept closing her eyes and raising her hands in the air during the songs. She had a particularly beautiful expression of peace and joy on her face, but then Robyn noticed that her hands had no fingers. The woman had had leprosy.

Later, when Robyn was meeting all the women, the woman told her through an interpreter that she was illiterate.

"I have never read the Bible but I love Jesus, and I listen carefully in church each week to the Scriptures as they are explained," she said. "I could never explain clearly enough to anyone about the Bible, but each week I bring one new person to church so they can hear about God for themselves."

Robyn asked the interpreter if this was so.

"Yes," she said, "and we don't know where she finds them!"

As well as meeting individuals, Robyn was working with larger groups too.

A conference in Tonga 1999 on evangelism brought together Pacific Islanders, New Zealanders and Australians.

On the last day, the Queen of Tonga took to the platform, urging everyone to come before Jesus in repentance, seeking his forgiveness and being reconciled with him. Then came a very memorable event. Delegates from each nation were asked to stand while one person brought her national flag and knelt at the foot of a large cross at the base of the stage.

When Tonga's turn came, the Queen came down from the platform. She took the flag and knelt humbly with it before the cross. It was moving for everyone, but especially for Tongans. Royal families are meant to be higher than everyone else, but here was the Queen kneeling before the cross while everyone stood behind her.

"We saw a Christian Queen prepared to forego her royal position, because, before the Cross of Christ, she was a daughter of the King of Kings," remembered Robyn. "Her actions were a sign that the words she had spoken were acted out in her life".[6]

Even larger groups gathered in different parts of the world. The conference in Houston in 2001, after September 11, brought together over 10,000 international Christian women to be encouraged in evangelism and ministry.

And Robyn was always there, organising, speaking and mentoring, and doing it all with her usual smile and energy. Even as Robyn got older, her energy did not seem to diminish. In fact, she said, in later life, that she has always felt about 35 years of age. So she may not have been so pleased to realise that the first impression some women had of her was of a "very elderly and senior person in the Christian community".[7] Evangeline Sita of India has a mental picture of her side by side with Dr Billy Graham. However, Evangeline's expectation that Robyn would be a very serious person, only interested in talking seriously to others her age, was quickly replaced.

"She could relate to all age groups, and not only on a superficial basis but being genuinely interested," wrote Evangeline later.

Eva Mrsic agreed. "She is a wonderful person to meet and work with," she wrote. "She makes everybody around her feel important, loved and welcome."

As usual, very few people ever saw Robyn down or depressed. "Even when she was almost exhausted, being so fragile in her physical body, her spirit was shining and was radiating energy,"

---

[6] That same year the Queen asked every woman in Tonga to share the good news of Jesus with every member of her family by the year 2000.

[7] According to Evangeline Sita, 2005.

wrote Olga Zaprometova. "These truths of the word of God – 'The joy of the Lord is our strength'[8] and 'His yoke is easy and His burden is light'[9] - are embodied in Robyn's personality."

But while she may have been appreciated, not everything had been positive and easy for Robyn in her new role. Her physical body was indeed fragile. As all conscientious women should, she was having regular medical checkups and routine mammograms. In 1998 when a small lump in her breast was discovered, Robyn had to have some further tests. The results came through while she and David were in the car on the way to the airport where she was to go to Germany to speak at a conference.

"I'm afraid the results of your mammogram aren't good," said her doctor. "The lump is malignant and you'll have to have an operation as soon as you can."

David prayed with Robyn in the car and they left it in God's hands. With a real sense of peace, Robyn continued on to Germany, spoke at the conference, and returned home to have the lump removed three weeks later. Thankfully the cancer had not spread and Robyn made a full recovery.[10] After nearly a week in hospital, she came out to attend the launch of her first book the very next day.

Robyn had always loved to tell a story, and it seemed a waste to keep to herself the many inspiring stories of people she had met on her travels. From the very beginning, she thought that sharing stories would be helpful in encouraging women to keep at the task of evangelism.

So in 1998 she wrote them down, together with insights and

---

[8] Nehemiah 8:10

[9] Matthew 11:30

[10] Six weeks after the operation Robyn needed to have a course of radiotherapy. "Daily visits to the hospital were an interruption to my life!" she said. However, she wisely took the advice of her doctor and took it easy, cancelling most speaking appointments during that time, apart from the CMS Summer School in Queensland at which David and she were both speaking.

encouragements from Scripture, in a book entitled 'Doors are for Walking Through'.[11]

And the stories have been timely for many. "Your book has been a sustenance and inspiration and came at a time I was in real need," wrote one reader in 2000.[12]

"I find stories like these enormously helpful – they tell me that all I've got to do is be faithful to God where I am, to be prayerful and to be faithful, and when opportunities come, to take them," Robyn said in 2000. "I find it encouraging that God isn't using super-talented people, he's just using ordinary people who are committed to him."[13]

Being faithful to God where she was sometimes included Australia and even Sydney! When Robyn left Abbotsleigh, she took on an additional responsibility of being on the honorary staff of St Andrew's Anglican Cathedral in Sydney's CBD. One challenge that jumped straight out at her was how to talk about Jesus to the growing numbers of people living in high rise city apartments. Security in many apartment blocks meant she couldn't just go and knock on doors.

She began to pray for a way in, and initially established a couple of contacts with women living in two of the buildings. She then asked them if she could have a coffee morning in their apartments and invite the neighbours. A few flyers under doors served as invitations, and some gatherings of women came about, with Robyn explaining the gospel over morning tea. This ministry continued to grow as new opportunities in other buildings arose.

More widely, around Australia, Robyn chaired the Australian Lausanne Committee – focusing particularly on training emerging leaders and establishing a younger women's network. Inviting

---

[11] *Doors are for Walking Through* was published in 1998 by SPCK Australia, and is currently in its third edition. *Keep Walking* was the sequel in 2001.

[12] Letter from Hilaria Dongalen, Philippines, 2000

[13] Interview from *Alive Magazine* August 2000.

younger and older women to her home for dessert, she would ask a few to share about their ministries and provide opportunities for people to get to know each other.

And then there was the speaking, to a whole variety of different groups.

"Thank you very much for your faithful ministry to us," came one letter. "Your message was so clear and at the same time substantial. God has spoken through you to many women, both to show them Christ and to challenge and encourage."[14]

CMS benefited enormously from Robyn's ability to share the Scriptures and encourage Christians.

"Robyn is one of the all-time best Summer School speakers," were words from a regular at the CMS Queensland conference.[15]

But CMS was also grateful for her teamwork with David in the whole of his role as Federal Secretary. "We are mindful that his ministry amongst us has been shared unstintingly by Robyn," were the appreciative words on David's retirement in 2002.[16]

Robyn certainly had a lot of energy, a great deal of talent and many God-given gifts. She may have had more than most other people will ever have. But she also took the many opportunities God gave her, to use those things to the full for his glory. And that was her advice to every woman she ever met through her wide ministry, no matter who they were.

"God calls us to be his person right where we are, even though where we are might seem limited in its scope for gospel-sharing," she said in 1995. "We need to pray that when opportunities come to witness to our faith in the Lord Jesus, we might be ready."[17]

[14] Letter from Dorothy Piper, March 2000
[15] Andrew Lake, letter 2002.
[16] Minute of Appreciation, CMS Federal Executive, 2002
[17] Lausanne Women's Network Newsletter June 1995

CHAPTER TWENTY FOUR

YOU CAN'T PLEASE ALL OF THE PEOPLE, ALL OF THE TIME

The most challenging night that David ever had overseas was not while he was with CMS – it was a Scripture Union visit to a village in the rural hills of Taiwan. David had been invited to preach at an Easter service[1] and a Taiwanese theological student came along to interpret for him.

After a long bus trip, the two walked into the jungle in the dark for about an hour, until they eventually came to the village and were welcomed by the pastor.

"You'll stay with me, and friends nearby have arranged for your evening meal," he said.

David and his translator were hungry and were sent next door for their dinner – an enormous bowl of plain noodles. That would have been fine, except for the chooks pecking around them. Chicken mess covered the floor and the smell made it difficult to eat.

David ate as much as he could, giving the rest to the translator when no-one was looking, and then the two went back to the pastor's house to sleep. The house was a single room with concrete walls and a dirt floor. In one corner, the pastor's two children were asleep on a two metre square patch of concrete. His wife woke them

---

[1] The Easter service turned out to be a colourful experience. David preached his line in English, the translator would speak it in Taiwanese and the pastor translated into the Taya language. By the time it was David's turn to give the next sentence he had almost forgotten what he was up to as he was distracted by all the activity going on in church. Mothers would feed their babies, then pass them along the pew. Everyone in the pew and those sitting in the pew behind would help wrap each baby in long colourful pieces of material. The children (who had already been to a children's church service) ran around the building which had no walls, playing with balls. Often a ball would come in, there would be a fight over it in the middle of the aisle and a father would come and give the fighting children a big slap, resulting in tears and more noise!

up, moved them to the dirt floor, and then threw a bucket of water over the concrete.

"You can lie down there to sleep," she told David and his translator.

Thankfully they were both tired and slept quite well, but they awoke next morning needing to use the facilities. David politely asked where an appropriate toilet spot would be, assuming it would be nearby bushes outside.

He was surprised when he was told there was a toilet next door. The lady of this house showed him proudly into her single room dwelling, which had a beautifully clean and shining pedestal sitting right in the middle of it.

While she stood there to see what David would do with it, he looked around and saw no drainage. So he thanked her politely: "It looks very nice", left and headed off to the bushes.

It wasn't the best overnight visit of all time. Thankfully, when his job at CMS required more overseas visiting, it was not as difficult. Staying with CMS missionaries was a lot more comfortable and they usually had functional plumbing!

A large part of David's job was to care pastorally for the missionaries while they were on the field. Things had moved on a lot since Lora had been a CMS missionary and had been expected to cope as best she could with any 'personal' problems!

David strengthened the CMS resolve to make pastoral care a priority.

Caring for missionaries kept them from burning out or leaving the field early for avoidable reasons. David visited, and arranged for the State Secretaries to visit missionaries on a rostered arrangement, so that they would see their missionaries on location and get to know their local context. Missionaries also had regular 'debriefings' when they returned to Australia, where they could talk, unload their concerns and joys and discuss the future.

David enjoyed this part of his job. In 1991, he wrote to prayer supporters, "This is a very satisfying as well as a stretching ministry."

It was certainly stretching. Just a few of the issues to work through with people included job descriptions, locations, language difficulties, children's health, children's education, housing options, work permits and immigration, personality clashes with local church leaders, personality clashes with other missionaries, depression and anxiety, political tensions, retirement options, cars and vehicles, births of babies, inflation and money problems, further study needs of missionaries and administrative difficulties with CMS itself.

It was a heavy load too. In 1989, in a two-month period, David had 25 'debriefing' sessions with returning missionaries[2]. And he spent at least three or four one-month periods visiting missionaries in North Australia and overseas, moving from place to place, spending one or two nights in each house.

A few times in the year, Robyn would accompany David on these visits. It helps for a woman missionary to have a woman to talk to, and Robyn's particular gifts in counselling and listening were greatly appreciated.

But the pastoral part of David's job, even with Robyn's help, became the part that elicited the most controversial responses!

As the saying goes, 'You can't please all of the people all of the time'. This turned out to be very true of CMS missionaries. When CMS was looking for David's replacement, these two comments were heard[3]:

"We want someone who was pastorally sensitive like David," *and* "We want someone who is more pastorally aware than David."

---

[2] John Menear's memories of some of these meetings are of David, with endless patience, working through the details, taking as long as it needed. Other times, usually when he was pressured from his workload, he would be more time-conscious. Interview 2005.

[3] By Peter Chiswell, former Chair of Federal Executive, from interview, 2005.

Some missionaries had marvellous experiences with him.

Frances Boland, in Japan, needed assurance at one stage that her work was actually having a positive contribution to gospel ministry. She felt that David and Robyn went out of their way to find out her need, talk with the appropriate people and then to make sure she knew that she was valued.

Even if Frances thought something was too trivial to talk about she found David and Robyn to be excellent listeners, giving wise and helpful advice and following up her concerns later on.

One of these seemingly unimportant concerns was the matter of a winter coat. Japan is a cold country, and Frances is a tall lady. A thick wool coat bought in Japan was out of her budget and she was out of the normal Japanese size range. David found out about this on a pastoral visit and arranged for Frances' sister to buy her a coat in Australia, and someone else to take it across to Japan.

"He even wrote to let me know the coat had been bought and when to expect its arrival," Frances said later, still appreciative.[4]

When the Mulherin family, with five noisy boys, were expecting the 'big boss' to their place in Argentina for a pastoral visit, they weren't sure what to expect. All they really knew of David was his image of being a fairly formal high achiever with high standards and a high level of intellect.

Their memory[5] is of a warm-hearted person, sitting in their lounge room in casual clothes with his bare feet comfortably positioned on the coffee table, talking and listening and reading the Bible with them.

The youngest Mulherin boy climbed over him, under him and around him with laughs, and he answered questions from the older boys with no sign of impatience or discomfort. Later in the visit, he let the boys take pictures of a horse show-jumping event, and mailed

[4] Letter from Frances Boland, 2005.
[5] Letter from Chris and Lindy Mulherin, 2005.

the photos back a few weeks later. The boys christened him 'DC Talks' after the popular Christian band because of the stories he told. Chris and Lindy felt closer to God and encouraged through his visit. The 'big boss' image they had held was quickly rejected.

Terry and Peter Blowes, also in Argentina, had a relationship with him which was more professional than personal. They appreciated the way he helped them think through their future needs and encouraged Peter to take a year off for more study.[6]

On the day of their first pastoral visit from him, they were in a flat panic with only three days before they left for Australia. David had taken an overnight bus across Argentina to get there, and arrived in the morning looking 'abnormally unshaven and dishevelled'! The Blowes had no time to let him freshen up, but shoved him into their old jeep while they ran around town in the blistering heat, doing their last minute chores so he could at least see their church and school.

Perhaps unsurprisingly, "He was very quiet," said Terry!

David was often very good at sorting out problems in ministry jobs, or dealing with local leaders who had differences with the missionaries. In France, Danny Mullins appreciated the insight and decisive action he showed in helping them "untangle some diplomatic knots".[7] He continued: "We were especially touched by the expression of the high value you place on gospel workers and on their care."[8]

But, of course, at the opposite end of the spectrum were some missionaries who did not share that view, and who felt under-valued and un-cared for.

On one visit, a missionary couple arrived back to their house with David after a long sweltering car trip to find their kitchen

---

[6] Letter from the Blowes, 2005.
[7] Letter 2002.
[8] Letter, 2002.

overrun with rats. The three of them chased the rats away and filled up the hole, whereupon David assumed that they would be ready to sit down and start talking together. Their memory of the event is feeling that David's interest was not in the immediate problem, but only in sitting and talking.

In another location, a missionary who had been sent to do a specific and well-publicised ministry, had left after a very short time for personal reasons. When David visited the area, he spent a lot of time trying to sort out the future of her ministry and the funding for the project with the local leaders. But the other missionaries in the same location felt he was more interested in that situation, and had passed over their work and their needs.

Why was David's pastoral ministry perceived in such different ways?

One reason may be that missionaries have different expectations. Alan Hohne said later: "I think almost all missionaries would have an unreasonable expectation of pastoral care."[9]

Another reason may be the short, 'passing through' nature of visits. It can take a long time for some people to open up, and David noticed that many people only really started to talk once the clock hit 11pm. For a pastoral visitor coping with travel tiredness, sleeping in different beds every night and eating different food every day, it could be a natural response to seem tired by the time the talking really gets going.

Personality differences,[10] or even philosophical or theological differences between David and missionaries, may have accounted for some of the reactions. And location may have played a part too. David clearly enjoyed being in the Middle East, and some people saw him as being ideally suited to the formality of relationships in

---

[9] Interview, 2005.

[10] John Menear's perception was that David seemed more comfortable engaging with people on an intellectual level. Interview 2005.

Japan[11], but his reactions to other places may not have been so positive.

The fact that David saw his visits as being useful in visiting more people than just the missionaries also didn't help. Everywhere he went, he tried to build bridges, make contacts and do ground work for possible openings. But missionaries, who may have expected all his time to be spent with them, may not have appreciated this dual focus.

One big problem was the structure of his job. As Federal Secretary, he carried the dilemma of being required to pastor and care for the missionaries, while at the same time having to negotiate with their local 'bosses', the church leaders, and occasionally, as the 'boss' from Australia, carry messages of rebuke or discipline, or just plain bad news.

One particularly bad piece of news came in 1992. CMS has always seemed to struggle with a lack of funds, and, in this extremely 'dry' year, all missionaries and staff were required to take a five percent reduction in allowances. David was the one responsible for communicating this to missionaries, who already were living on minimal incomes. It cannot have improved his standing with those he visited soon after!

But the reality is that missionaries are people. People see things differently, depending on their expectations, their backgrounds, their previous experiences, their current situations and the mood of the day.

And people, as human beings, will always have emotional reactions. Those missionaries, who had positive emotional reactions about David and Robyn, were more than willing to share their experiences for this book. Missionaries who had negative emotional reactions to David's pastoral ministry often had trouble pinpointing or articulating the problem in detail.

---

[11] According to Alan Hohne, 2005.

Bill Graham believed that, generally, most missionaries enjoyed having him in their homes and benefited from his counsel and friendship. "He was fallible," he said, "however, given the dimensions of the job David held, he gets a good pass mark as a pastor. I would say seven out of ten, and no-one gets ten except Jesus."[12]

The fact remained, that even if some missionaries did not personally appreciate David's pastoral care, the structures of that pastoral care were improved considerably during David's time at CMS.

In previous years, it had been a regular thing to have a first-term missionary or family 'crash and burn', and have to return home permanently to Australia, according to Alan Hohne.

"Now it's the exception," he said. "We're aware of everybody who might be in real difficulty before they get to the point of giving up.[13]"

Formal debriefings and annual 48-hour visits by CMS staff to missionaries on the field now helped to do something about the problems, rather than committees simply bemoaning the fact after a missionary resigned broken-hearted.

There were other structural changes that needed to be made too. In Lora's day, the missionary organization had been the all-powerful authoritarian group at home, making decisions for missionaries such as where they would work, when they would travel, and even if they could get married.

Things had moved on, but CMS's decision-making ability was still controlled by very conservative policy guidelines which took lengthy debates to change. For example, if a missionary wanted to go into a new area because there was a window of opportunity for evangelism, it could have taken several years to get approval. David

[12] Letter, 2005.
[13] Interview 2005.

brought a new flexibility to guidelines and policy which allowed quicker decision-making, and gave more options to the missionaries themselves. Despite being older than many of the people he was working with, he had an openness to new ideas, and was quick to challenge the status quo.[14]

He also tried to get away from the concepts of CMS being a legal organisation and wanting missionaries to obey the rules. He was more interested in writing a guideline: "Here is the principle for us to follow" than creating regulations: "You shall not".

The fourteen years as Federal Secretary were busy, tiring, rewarding, challenging and joyful. David was well-appreciated, and well spoken of by the majority of people around him, but one incident had the potential to cloud his last few years.

Ross Hall, as Personnel Secretary, had worked closely with David in the Federal Office for many years.[15] Their relationship had been happy from David's point of view. However, when Ross was asked to move on from CMS by the Executive Committee[16], David was seen by some to be part of it. The issue became personal and complicated and was difficult for everyone involved.

But by 2002 retirement was quickly approaching for David, and people were beginning to look back on what he had achieved under God.

CMS had moved into the new era, with a good reputation for gospel ministry. It had a wider support base, a clearly defined Vision and a reputation for pastoral care of its missionaries.

---

[14] According to John Menear, 2005.

[15] The Personnel Secretary dealt with more of the practical issues missionaries faced on the field, and shared in the pastoral visiting. Ross Hall particularly focused on East Africa as he had been a missionary there for many years.

[16] Peter Chiswell and Alan Hohne, of the CMS Federal Executive committee, were both very clear in 2005 that it was the Executive's decision to ask Ross Hall to step down. After an initial conversation with Ross, David was not involved in any more meetings or decisions about it.

David's own style in what was 'an enormously difficult job' was appreciated as being careful, professional and godly.[17] He and Robyn had again shown trust in God and support of each other, graciously enduring long separations, and often uncomfortable travel, to do faithfully the task God had given them.

"David has clearly been God's man for the times," wrote Bill Graham on David's retirement. "I have no doubt that history will demonstrate that he assumed the leadership of CMS Australia at a critical time in both church and mission history."

And as for Alan Hohne, so carefully holding in his glee at St Matthew's all those years ago, was he content with the outcome of what he helped do in getting David to CMS?

His answer: "Unequivocally."

---

[17] Peter and Terry Blowes, 2002

CHAPTER TWENTY FIVE

SEEING ONLY HIM

Lora Claydon's life and work came to an end on 10 June 1985. She had had for years a great expectation that Jesus would return soon, but her turn to go to meet her beloved God and Saviour came first.

After some strokes, Lora had to move to a high care unit, but she was unwilling to do it until David and Robyn persuaded her it was for the best. The nursing staff knew that only David was the one who could move her.

"She'll do whatever you ask her to do," they said. "She needs to move. Would you persuade her?"

It was not a long time of suffering for Lora. She was never really aware of the effect of the strokes she had, and, after a period of unconsciousness, she passed quickly away.

David and Robyn mourned her loss. They had been on loving, close terms with her for many years, and she had grown to love them more as well. But still, David's memories of Lora remained bittersweet.

Of course, she had saved his life and provided for him. He was very conscious of these blessings which had come through her. But he was still hurt by the sufferings and loss he had felt at her hand. The difficulty was to reconcile both the thankfulness and pain he felt about their relationship.

It was only some years after her death that David realized he was still harbouring sin in his heart, by holding onto the bitterness that had grown up around the memory of his 'Aunty Lora'. With God's help, he was able to deeply forgive her, and appreciate fully what she had done for him.

More grief came when Robyn's father, Ronald Hickin, passed away after a short illness in 1988, aged 76. Madelon Hickin died in similar circumstances five years later, aged 83. Robyn and David felt the sadness of losing them; for David they had been the loving Christian family he had wanted so much to belong to. However, they had a great peace because they knew they were both now with the Lord they had loved so much. Robyn counted it a privilege to conduct both of their funeral services.

But even while some lives come to an end, new lives are just beginning. For Robyn and David, it was a true joy, with Kim and David, to welcome their grandchildren, Andrew and Georgia, into the world in the early 1990s. Living close by, they have been part of the children's growing up, seeing them often, and spending a holiday with them each year.

As might be expected for such international travellers, Robyn's and David's favourite memories of their grandchildren are not situated in Sydney. They look back fondly on Andrew as a two year-old chasing pigeons in St Mark's Square in Venice, while being photographed by Japanese tourists, and of making flower leis with Georgia in Hawaii.

Seeing their growing faith has been a great joy to David and Robyn. Andrew, when interviewed at his confirmation service in June 2005, said how grateful he was to be born into a Christian family. Georgia, in 2004, wrote: "Dear Heavenly Father, I thank you for my parents, they are so wonderful. Please help more people to become Christians and to love you. I thank you that my family and I love you so much. I pray this all in Jesus' name."[1]

Robyn's beloved sister Marlene and her family have remained close, despite living in the UK. Robyn and David have travelled the length and breadth of Britain with Marlene as a result.

---

[1] This prayer is pinned to the noticeboard in the Barker family kitchen

Much of the Claydon's extensive international travel schedule came to an end once David retired from CMS, in 2002, at the age of 65.[2] However, his retirement was never going to be all golf and gardening. Before leaving CMS, he had already received a number of invitations for work.

One was to be an honorary consultant to CMS on Islam, setting up a strategy group known as the *Islamic Awareness Task Force*.

Another was to be the International Director of Lausanne. This invitation was for three years, leading up to the fourth big international conference organized by Lausanne, 'The Forum', which was held in Thailand in 2004. Over 1,500 Christian leaders gathered from 130 different countries for seven days of discussion, encouragement and fellowship. This time, 600 women attended and contributed significantly!

It was an enormous job, and Roger Parrott, the treasurer and Forum Director, believes David and Robyn went beyond what would normally be called a 'tireless effort' to make the Forum happen.

"They gave up their life for two years in order to make it possible," he said.[3] "For months the Christian world intersected around their kitchen table, as they linked together leaders all over the globe to focus on the most critical issues for the Church in the years ahead. They poured themselves into this task as no one else would have, and, without their complete effort, the Forum would not have come about."

Robyn was the official Program Chair, responsible, with a committee, for the overall planning and the content of the Forum[4],

---

[2] David and Robyn still accept invitations for up to three trips a year. The long flights are 'tedious', but they use the time for reading and writing, and see the travel as the means of getting to countries with lots of opportunities for ministry and meeting people who enrich their lives.

[3] Email from Dr Roger Parrott, 2005.

[4] Robyn's Lausanne commitments continued. In 2001she was asked to serve on Lausanne International Committee as Vice-chairperson.

which had the theme, 'A new Vision, a New Heart and a Renewed Call'. She and David worked together to choose leadership teams of five people from around the world for each of the 31 Issue Groups, and set up the purpose of and expected outcomes of each Group. David also had to make the tough decisions about which participants qualified for financial assistance to attend, and get visas for all the delegates from African countries. As usual, David roped in his friends and contacts to help. Harold Dews was recruited to give his assistance in the visa gathering, and was impressed to see how compassionate yet decisive, David could be in making the scholarship decisions.[5]

"They did the work that would have easily taken five paid staff members to cover, and they did it without ever accepting a single dime for their efforts," said Parrott.

At the conference itself, Robyn hosted the opening welcome dinner and was one of the plenary Bible study speakers. As a chairperson, she also had to keep the speakers and panellists in line with the schedule. All the main speakers and panellists had been given very strong instructions about their time limits to speak, and would not be allowed one minute longer than their allotted time. But on the last evening David got up to speak.

"It was excellent," remembered Eva Mrsic[6], who was in the audience, "but his time passed by."

Some of the Forum officials sitting in the first row started to telegraph signs to David that he should finish, but David couldn't see them.

Eva saw Robyn sitting behind him, aware of the situation, and thinking what to do.

"After a while, I saw her slowly standing and gently walking to her husband, putting her hand behind his back and with some

[5] Interview with Harold Dews, 2005.
[6] Email from Eva Mrsic 2005.

words letting him know that his time was way over," she said. "It was funny and nice to see how she wisely and gently handled the situation."

At the Forum, David, who had been held 'in enormous regard' by the Lausanne delegates[7], handed over his International Directorship to Dr Ted Yamamori, and came home with Robyn to still more work for Lausanne, editing the 31 Issue Group papers, a full-time job for nearly a year.[8]

Since then, David has helped out in a few Sydney parishes and has conducted an appraisal of a Sydney parish. He accepts speaking engagements around Sydney and in different parts of Australia, with a particular interest in speaking about Islam. David also continues to enjoy his work as a Governor of The Kings School, Parramatta. He has big plans to write a book on 'identity' when he finally gets the time.

Robyn has not retired from her International Lausanne women's ministry, and continues with her young women's Mentor network in Sydney, as well as mentoring young Christian teachers. She still leads the Women's Bible Study at St Andrew's Cathedral, and reaches out to women who live in Sydney's CBD.

But even energetic Robyn had to slow down a little sometime. After 13 years as Chair of the Australian Lausanne Committee she handed the position over in July 2005 to Dr Ross Clifford, Principal of the Baptist Church's Morling College.

However, like David, she continues to speak around Australia, particularly for CWCI, Christian Women Communicating International, and is still appreciated by the women who hear her. She also preaches in churches and speaks at various school Speech Days, and visits William Clarke College, at Kellyville in Sydney,

---

[7] According to Harold Dews, interview 2005.
[8] The edited papers are now on the Lausanne website and are being printed as a two volume compendium.

each year to speak to the 'Claydon House' students.[9] With good responses from her first two books,[10] Robyn is now working on her next book.

They enjoy catching up with old friends in and out of Australia, and they have loved spending more time together working, speaking and travelling. David's extensive coin collection[11] has benefited from his extra time, and he and Robyn try to expand their shared interest in archaeology by visiting digs and ruins when they travel. With good health and plenty of interests and invitations, life has plenty for them to look forward to.

If David, at the age of 16, in tears every night and suffering badly from loneliness, had been able to look forward and see what God had in store for him, he would have been amazed.

But all he could do at that age was to continue in faith that God had his life in the palm of His hand. He could only trust that God knew him, that God cared about him, and that he would never be alone. It was a trust that was not misplaced.

When, much later in life, he shared a detailed memoir of his childhood experiences with a few close friends, they were able to look back at what his life had been, and were astounded by God's goodness to him.

"It's a story that wrenches at the heart – several times – but it is also glorious, in God's peculiar way," wrote his sister-in-law, Marlene, in response.

Ron Winton, David's good friend and mentor from his formative years at Wingham, wrote: "I can only say, in complete sincerity and without any sanctimoniousness, that any good done at Wingham was by the grace of God. What you have written sheds a lot of light on what happened to you in those days... God has given you an

---

[9] Claydon House was named after Robyn.

[10] *Doors are for Walking Through* and *Keep Walking*.

[11] As well as more recent coins, David has a few coins from the time of Christ, and an ancient Chinese coin from 700 BC which he will gladly tell interested people about.

amazing life-education for what He has led you into today, and for what He may have in store for you in the future. He has been very close to you from the earliest days of your life, whether or not you were aware of it."[12]

Colin Becroft was a little more blunt.[13] "You should have been a psychological wreck!" he said. "By the grace of God you are not!"

By the grace of God, both Robyn and David look back on their lives with joy: joy at the gifts given to them, joy at the many opportunities to use their gifts, and joy at the many ways in which they have seen those gifts build up their brothers and sisters in Christ.

Life has been happy, enriching, fun and stimulating. And they, in turn, have been touched and enriched, both by their immediate family and by the many members of their Christian family, whose lives have touched theirs.

All their lives, they have been mindful of the God who has saved them, the Christ who has captured their hearts and the Spirit who dwells in them. And they have tried, in response to God's grace, to echo in their lives the words of the hymn that was sung at their wedding:

May the mind of Christ my Saviour,
Live in me from day to day,
By His love and power controlling
All I do and say.

May His beauty rest upon me
As I seek the lost to win,
And may they forget the channel
Seeing only Him.

[12] Ron Winton's letter to David, October 1995.
[13] In his letter of March 2000.

BIBLIOGRAPHY

Claydon, David	*Only Connect* 1993 Lancer, ANZEA Publishers, Australia
Claydon, David (ed)	*Scripture Union: Towards an Australian Centenary* 1975, Scripture Union Australia
Claydon, Robyn	*Me? A Success? Living Skills for Teenagers* 1989 ANZEA Bookhouse (distributors) Australian
Cohen, Marlene	*The Divided Self* 1996 Marshall Pickering, London
Hawkins, Doris	*Atlantic Torpedo* 1943, Victor Gollancz Ltd, London
Lutz, Lorry	*Looking forward to the rest of your life?* 2004, Baker Books, Grand Rapids, USA
Piggin, Stuart	*Spirit of a Nation* 2004 Strand Publishing, Sydney
Prince, John, Moyra	*Tuned Into Change* 1979 Scripture Union Australia
Sylvester, Nigel	*God's Word in a young world: the story of Scripture Union* 1984 Scripture Union International Council, London

INDEX